MASTERING THE ART OF COMMUNICATION

A Happy Thoughts Initiative

MASTERING THE ART OF COMMUNICATION
By WOW Publishings Pvt. Ltd.

Copyright © Tejgyan Global Foundation
All Rights Reserved 2021

Tejgyan Global Foundation is a charitable organization
with its headquarters in Pune, India.

ISBN : 978-93-90607-23-5

Published by WOW Publishings Pvt. Ltd., India

First edition published in May 2021

Printed and bound by Trinity Academy, Pune, INDIA

Copyrights are reserved with Tejgyan Global Foundation and publishing rights are vested exclusively with WOW Publishings Pvt. Ltd. This book is sold subject to the condition that it shall not by way of trade or otherwise, be lent, resold, hired out, or otherwise circulated without the publisher's prior written consent in any form of binding or cover other than that in which it is published and without a similar condition including this condition being imposed on the subsequent purchaser and without limiting the rights under copyright reserved above, no part of this publication may be reproduced, stored in or introduced into a retrieval system, or transmitted, in any form, or by any means, electronic, mechanical, photocopying, recording or otherwise, without the prior written permission of both the copyright owner and the above-mentioned publisher of this book. Any person who does any unauthorized act in relation to this publication may be liable to criminal prosecution and civil claims for damages.

Although the author and publisher have made every effort to ensure accuracy of content in this book, they hereby disclaim any liability to any party for any loss, damage, or disruption caused by errors or omissions, resulting from negligence, accident, or any other cause. Readers are advised to take full responsibility to exercise discretion in understanding and applying the content of this book.

*To those
who have attained
mastery in the art of communication
and helped people gain proficiency
in this fine art to achieve lasting success.*

Contents

	Preface	7
	PART 1 - FROM MISCOMMUNICATION TO GOOD COMMUNICATION	**13**
1.	Steering Clear of Miscommunication	17
2.	Becoming a Better Listener	25
3.	Using the Right Words	35
4.	Gentleness in Speech	43
5.	Expressing that You Care	47
	PART 2 - DEEPER NUANCES OF COMMUNICATION	**51**
6.	Appreciating and Complimenting	55
7.	Caring about Others' Self-image	60
8.	Would you be Right or Rather be Happy?	67
9.	Criticism is of No Help	71
10.	Critiguiding – Part 1	76
11.	Critiguiding – Part 2	80

	PART 3 - COMMUNICATION IN THE FAMILY	**85**
12.	Forming a Platform for Communication	87
13.	Glass Breaking	96
14.	Feeling Secure in Communication	101
15.	Connecting with People	106
	PART 4 - THE SIX KEYS TO SUCCESSFUL COMMUNICATION	**111**
Key 1	Asking the Right Questions	115
Key 2	Being Respectfully Candid	120
Key 3	Sticking to the Topic	128
Key 4	Saying "No"	137
Key 5	Having Difficult Conversations Gracefully	142
Key 6	Saying the Unsaid	149
	Self-Review through Introspection	158

Preface

A school was conducting a game of Dumb Charades to help children improve their communication skills. In this game, one has to enact a word, phrase, or the name of a movie to one's partner or team. While doing so, one is not allowed to use any words or sounds. One has to do this entirely with the help of gestures, wordlessly!

A bowl full of chits with various words written on them was placed before the children. Each child, on his or her turn, would pick one chit and enact the word written on it, and the rest would need to guess it. Now the challenge with this game was the rule that disallows the use of speech. The children had to rely entirely on their skill to enact the word, to communicate it to the rest. So now, each child would get up and enact the word that was written on their chit. Someone would try acting like a taxi, someone would be a plane, someone a kite, and someone would endeavor to enact a multiplex cinema!

Each child was trying to communicate something about the word they had picked to the rest, but funnily enough, the remaining children were finding it difficult to grasp what was being communicated. They were making all the wrong guesses. The ones trying to enact the words felt that their audience was giving all but the one correct answer; and this was making them angry and discouraged.

We have all played this game at some time, haven't we? Sometimes, we successfully communicate the right thing to our playmates, but sometimes we fail! Indeed, this being a book about communication, the example of dumb charades is an apt one. But other than the fact that dumb charades is a game about communication, there is another interesting parallel here.

Unlike the game, our daily communication thankfully doesn't have to follow the rule of 'not speaking'. And yet, the outcome of our communication is not very different from that of the game! Even with the full use of our ability to speak and with a fair vocabulary at our disposal, we still fail to get people to understand what we're trying to say. Not that this is always the case. Sometimes we do succeed in getting through, but sometimes the other person extracts their own meaning of our words, which is entirely different from what we meant to convey.

And thus, ensues the familiar struggle due to strained relationships, broken bonds, misunderstandings, and even distrust.

Today, this is even more applicable to written online communication on the various messaging platforms. There are countless instances of communication gone wrong through these mediums. These platforms allow us to send written messages, but often the tone or intent of the message is not conveyed, leading to confusion and miscommunication. Text written in newspapers and online blogs is always subject to misinterpretation, leading to miscommunication on a massive scale.

Being a proficient communicator entails mastering the art of communication to such a degree, that you can always communicate exactly what you mean to say—no more, no less—without giving miscommunication a chance.

Have you noticed that everything in nature—from the sun to the mountains, from the breeze to the animals and insects—is communicating something all the time? Think about it. The sun rises in the morning—an unspoken message for everyone to wake up and get about. Animals cannot speak, and yet they can perfectly communicate with their young ones and also others of their species. Interestingly, they are immune to miscommunication! What a beautiful system nature has evolved through them! Saying everything without having to say a word!

Humans—the only race that God chose to give the ability to think and speak! We can think and contemplate others' words. We are given the gift of language to present our ideas and thoughts to others. And yet, if we were to look around and observe carefully, we will undoubtedly hear statements like:

"He is such a brat! Doesn't have the basic decency to speak properly!"

"God... does she ever stop talking?! Everyone at her home must be mute and deaf!"

"Who the hell is he to tell me how things are to be done? And so rudely too!"

"I'll never trust a word that he says... he's always blowing his own trumpet!"

We, too, may have said such things about others at times. All this is due to the lack of effective communication.

Several candidates appear for interviews, and yet only a handful get selected. Why? Communication! Many candidates may have a lot to say, but they are unable to say it right. One thing is said, something altogether different is understood, and in the end, the interviewer thinks, "I don't think he knows what he is talking about," and rejection! This is especially true for technical jobs. The person might be an expert at the technical skill required for the job, but due to poor communication skills, he simply fails to convince his interviewer that he is an expert.

This is like someone building a magnificent house with all the luxuries and beautiful interiors, and then forgetting to make a door to enter the house! Of what use is all that expertise if one cannot convey the expertise to others?! If people could also work on their communication skills, they'll have no problem getting selected, even for their dream job!

Such instances of great losses due to miscommunication can be seen everywhere—between friends, in offices, in relations, and in the world of online communication. Hence, it is imperative that we get to work on our communication skills as soon as we can, and that is exactly what this book is all about. Surely, we will all agree that in today's age, words—whether written or spoken—are the most important carriers of our communication, and that is what a major portion of this book explores.

It is an age-old saying that "Words can make or break a relationship." So today, let us begin our journey towards mastering the art of communication by learning the best techniques there are. Let us understand the world of words and make them our friends, so that we may use them wisely and positively to make our lives and of those around us, infinitely better!

Better communication does not mean one has to talk more, thereby simply increasing the number of words one uses, nor does it mean using smarter jargons. Learning the art of communication entails learning how, when, where, and how much to say. Whatever it is that one wants to tell the other person, there is an appropriate *way* of saying it.

Which words should we pick?

Which moment should we choose to speak and when do we choose to stay quiet?

How long should we take to convey what we want to?

Which location should we choose to meet?

As we begin thinking about all the above questions and understanding their implications, we begin our journey on the path to mastering the art of communication. Communication is successful only when our listener(s) understand exactly what we want to say.

It doesn't help to always speak our ideas or thoughts, exactly the way they pop up in our minds. It is necessary to also use some logical intelligence to articulate them properly, depending on the situation we are in and the kind of audience we have. Anyone who blurts out anything and everything that pops up in their mind, exactly as it pops up, is sooner or later termed as insane by society—however intelligent they may be.

We have heard stories of brilliant scientists being branded as insane and outcast by society, simply because they could not articulate their words well. The part of their brain that filters and articulates their communication is dormant, leading to communication failure. So many artists excel at their art but are a disaster when it comes to communication.

Hence, even if a person is skilled, intelligent, and resourceful within, the lack of communication skills will soon get him struggling to grow in his chosen field of activity. The very purpose of speech is for us to be able to interact with others. If this goal is not being met, it is time for us to work on it.

Just like we learn to correctly use punctuations like commas, semicolons, and full-stops to produce well-written prose, it is equally necessary to correctly use vocabulary, voice modulation, and body language, to produce a well-said and a well-understood sentence. This is good communication and it has to be learned as an art. To learn it, one has to practice it perseveringly, the way one would if one is learning how to swim. This practice is necessary because just like any other art, it cannot be taught; one has to teach oneself.

If someone wants to learn swimming, the coach will teach techniques and even monitor them while they apply the techniques. But finally, the onus lies with the learner to master the skill through practice. Likewise, with communication, external guidance can be acquired from sources like this book, but it is up to the learner to practice the techniques and master the art.

To begin with, contemplate on the following questions every night:

- Who all did I interact with today?
- Did I feel anything wrong about the conversation? Was the person left with a sad, discouraged, angry, or any other negative feeling after speaking with me?
- Did I use any wrong or inappropriate words?
- What better words or ways of articulation could I have employed to say the same things to the person?
- How was my body language while I was conversing?

As we form a habit of contemplating this way, we will soon notice that our contemplation begins immediately after the conversation, probably even during the conversation, making us change our demeanor instantaneously! Contemplation will become a part of the activity, not something to be done later. That is the beauty of contemplation; it assimilates itself into whatever one does!

The fifteen techniques and six keys for empathetic and assertive communication described in this book, along with our contemplation and rigorous practice, will certainly put us on the track to master this beautiful art! Let us begin with the first section of the book.

PART 1

FROM MISCOMMUNICATION TO GOOD COMMUNICATION

The Golden Rule

After his defeat, when Porus was held captive and brought before Alexander, the latter asked him how he wished to be treated. To that, Porus held his head high and replied, "Treat me like a king would treat another king!"

This little incident between Porus and Alexander, which we all would have heard of, is an example of the Golden Rule, that states, **"Treat people the way you would want them to treat you."** Everyone wants to be treated with love, kindness, and respect. We all feel that when people talk to us, they should do so in respectful and pleasant words; that they should behave gently and sweetly with us.

When the same rule is understood more deeply in the spiritual context, it becomes: **"Treat people with the understanding of who they really are, for you would want them to treat you with the same understanding."**

We all consider ourselves and others as separate individuals, as the "I", the ego. In the context of spirituality, we make statements like, **"The same God resides in all of us," "We all are one and the same in essence,"** and so on. But these words have somehow lost their experiential meaning. Their existence has been reduced to mere words, repeated generation after generation, without their essential meaning being understood by the greater mass of people. The real Self has become shrouded by the illusory self and this illusory self has been unknowingly adopted as our identity. We perceive ourselves and everyone else as this limited "I". We need to look at and treat others and ourselves as the real Self—beyond limitations and personalities.

But then, the question arises: "Who is the real Self? What is the real Self like?" Finding answers to such questions through direct experience is the crux of spirituality. When one is in the purest, most tranquil, innocent, most peaceful and loving state, just like how a little child is—that—is our real Self. Consider how kids are. If we were to write down all the adjectives that describe children, we are likely to end up with a list of words like innocent, loving, trusting, peaceful, beautiful, tranquil, carefree, joyful, and so on. Not surprisingly, all these adjectives apply to the real Self.

Children *are* the real Self. The experience of the real Self is very much alive and projecting in and through them. Children are full of love, inner peace, and joy. They look at everyone with the same love, peace, and joy, not differentiating anyone on any basis. For them, everyone is beautiful, just as they are. Whoever interacts with them, whether ugly or beautiful, rich or poor, old or young, their response is undifferentiated. They do not even recognize such labels as ugly, beautiful, rich, poor, old, young, etc. These labels come into play later in their lives.

As they grow up, the experience of the real Self, which was so clear when they were infants, slowly fades away as dust accumulates over it—the dust of conditioning of the mind, the ego. Like a dirty pair of spectacles, this layer of dust also shrouds their eyesight. The eyes that could only see good in others, now begin to see negatives, flaws and shortcomings.

However, when we practice meditation and dwell in inner silence—not by being quiet and saying nothing, but by silencing the egoistic mind—we slowly begin to realize the presence of our real Self. The experience that had gotten shrouded over the years, starts coming back to us and we start looking at everyone the way an infant does. We see the same goodness, honesty and beauty in everyone. With this improved vision, our interactions with people naturally become pleasant, sweet, empathetic and respectful.

The very fact that we understand who the other person really is, changes our behavior.

1
Steering Clear of Miscommunication

Let's get one thing straight—it is impossible for us to not communicate at all!

Be it through body language, speech, gestures, or a combination of these, we are constantly communicating. We are saying something even when we are not actually saying anything. It is because of such silent communication and the tendency of presuming things, that miscommunication takes root, leading to souring of relationships. This could happen inadvertently or otherwise.

One fine day, an employee noticed that his boss was tense and wasn't speaking to him. From his boss's body language, he presumed that his boss was upset with him for some reason and felt offended, thereby souring their relationship. His boss could have been upset about a horde of other things, totally unrelated to the employee, but his tendency to presume made the employee concoct his own story about his boss's behavior without trying to find the truth.

This is the age of digital entertainment and we are seeing the release of a plethora of web-series and films. A lot of these portray characters who advertently or inadvertently cause miscommunication. Besides deriving entertainment, it is good to use our time to study such characters and incidences to make sure we do not make such mistakes in our lives.

In a particular film, two friends had stopped connecting with each other due to some miscommunication. They couldn't look at each other in the eye. Then one day, one of the friends wrote an email to the other—a long explanatory email in which he presented his side of things in positive and respectful words. He even wrote his complaints about his friend, but in the same respectful manner. The other friend took this communication in the right spirit and the two friends came together again. We too can adopt their method of overcoming misunderstandings.

Written communication can do wonders, especially in cases where verbal communication doesn't seem to work. In fact, written communication even helps in strengthening relationships. Consider the tradition of giving greeting cards to family members, friends, and colleagues at work, on various occasions. In addition to verbally wishing people, offering greeting cards is a warm way of telling them how we regard them and how much we love them. A spoken word may be forgotten over time, but a written word will arouse the same feeling every time it is read. It is like a record that lasts a long time.

If one purposely tries to be deceitful, exaggerating, or understating, thereby mis-representing the truth about something, the other person can possibly become angry and frustrated. And it doesn't stop there. When such things happen at the workplace among colleagues or at home within the family, this sentiment spreads to others. The train that begins with miscommunication between two people soon spreads to others as well. Many people fall prey to such incidents of miscommunication causing ruptures in loving relationships.

Let us now look at the most common reasons for miscommunication and how they can be avoided.

Reason 1 – Disparate definitions

The human mind has a tendency of viewing everything in the light of its own conditioned perspective. In other words, we judge everything we see, read or hear, to form a personalized definition of it all. For example, if a person sees a square pizza for the first time, he finds it impossible to believe it to be a pizza. Based on his past conditioning, he presumes that a pizza should be round. It is only when he is made to eat it that he agrees that it is in fact a pizza, only different in shape.

Likewise, when one says some words, he does so from his personal point of reference with his definitions of those words in mind. But the listeners may have their own different references and personalized definitions of those same words, and this gives rise to miscommunication.

For example, while the usual habit is to call one's parents 'Mum', 'Mother', 'Ma', 'Mom' or 'Dad', 'Father', 'Papa' and so on. Some people call their parents by their name. Finding this unusual, others judge them as lacking respect for their parents. But this is not necessarily true. Everyone has their own way of showing respect; their definition of respect for their parents may not involve calling them the way the rest of the world does. But this difference in definitions causes miscommunication.

A ten-year old boy gulped down half a glass of milk and cried out happily, "I am an optimist. My glass is half empty!"

"Seeing a glass as half empty is a sign of pessimism, not optimism, son!", corrected his father.

"Not if you don't like what's in it!" replied the son.

Now this is a joke, but it goes to show how the same words can mean different things to different people. The son was being optimistic while saying that his glass was half empty because he didn't like milk. His definition of the word was linked to his dislike of milk. However, his father looked at the word with the commonly accepted definition and hence the miscommunication!

Both the examples cited above, although simple, give us an insight into how people fall victim to miscommunication due to disparate definitions. Hence, it is important not to just focus on the words and get stuck with them, but to go beyond them and understand the point of reference from which they have been spoken.

Reason 2 – Wrong information

Sometimes people, either purposely or inadvertently spread wrong information. They are either themselves misinformed about something or do it purposely. In either case, the person who receives wrong information can suffer the consequences. A certain piece of information may not be very critical or important to the speaker but could be crucial for the listener. By not communicating it, the speaker does a disservice to the listeners.

For example, while delivering a training about repairing a certain gadget, a trainer forgets to mention a particular step that his trainees have to perform before they start. From the trainer's perspective it is a very simple and trivial step, but that's because he has spent years repairing the gadget. However, the new trainees have to be specifically directed to perform the step as they are new to the entire process. As we can see, the trainer is responsible for the miscommunication due to incomplete information, inadvertently though. We should hence make a practice to deliver complete and correct information while communicating, especially in critical situations where others' safety or reputation is at stake.

Reason 3 – Presumptions

This is an obscure reason that has been one of mankind's worst diseases—presumption. We often jump to conclusions by believing that our own version of things is right.

A father and his son were once sitting in the drawing room of their home, the father reading a newspaper and the son working on his laptop. A little later, the son's little sister entered the drawing room with two apples. She placed one apple on a table, wiped the other apple clean and bit into it. Pointing at the apple on the table, her brother said to her, "Would you give dad the other apple?" The girl picked up that apple too, wiped it clean, and bit into that too! The brother got angry at her, thinking how selfish she had been and was just about to scold her when the girl handed their father the first apple and said to him, "Dad, eat this one; it is sweeter than the other one." Her brother looked away, ashamed at himself for presuming the worst about his sister.

It is a human tendency to jump to conclusions finding out whether what they have understood is right.

A woman was very excited about her marriage anniversary. She called her husband at his workplace and asked him to come home early. The husband promised her, but the day passed by and he was still not home. The wife was upset and thought to herself, "I knew it. I'm the only one excited about this day." Looking at all her preparations made her even more upset and angry. Finally, the doorbell rang, and she opened the door to find her husband standing at the door with a box of cake and a huge bouquet of red roses in his hands. "Sorry darling," he said, "the florist took too long to deliver the roses that I had specially ordered!". The wife hugged him tight, feeling bad about what she had thought.

When an incident occurs, we fail to accept it as it is. We often dress it up with our presumptions and feelings about it. As a result, the event appears distorted, different to what it truly is, sometimes the very opposite! This illusion that we unhesitatingly accept as the absolute truth, breaks only when the complete picture becomes clear to us. But very often, by the time we realize it, it is already too late.

In the examples above, the brother and the wife both presumed their own version of truths, only to realize later how wrong they were. Thankfully, even though a little later, they do see the whole picture. In some cases, people never get to see the whole picture and they live with their illusory version of the truth all their lives. There are countless instances of relationships that implode and stay broken for life due to such presumptions, that could have been easily cleared, given a chance.

Therefore, it is important to not jump to conclusions based on half the picture. Only after the whole truth has been revealed should one contemplate on how to respond.

Reason 4 – Poor listening

Another major reason for miscommunication is poor listening, which happens advertently or otherwise.

Suppose someone is speaking to us and we are either thinking about what we will say next or our attention is elsewhere. We fail to listen to what the person is telling us. Conversely, if we have explained something to someone, we just assume that he or she has perfectly understood what we intended to say, without confirming it. Both these scenarios, cause miscommunication.

Chapter 2 deals with this aspect of deep listening, but to make a quick note here, a lot of people lack the skill of listening properly. And when one doesn't listen, one doesn't participate fully in the conversation.

There could be two reasons why a person cannot recall information from a conversation. Either he has forgotten it, or the piece of information never registered in his memory because he wasn't listening. Hence, when the information has to be applied at some later point, it cannot be recalled.

Reason 5 – Avoidance

In the endeavor to evade a drizzle, people often end up inviting a storm. Consider a mother who witnesses her son stealing money from his father's wallet. Ideally, she should stop him there and then. However, she refrains from confronting him, thinking that her teenage son might take offence and retaliate in an extreme way. She doesn't speak to the father about this either, fearing that he would scold their son. Although the mother has acted out of care for her son, she has avoided communicating about a small problem only to create a bigger one. This is like an expensive way of saving petty cash!

The son could develop the habit of stealing and finally get confronted about it in front of the whole family with a lot of embarrassment and admonishment. Had the mother communicated to her son at the first instance, the bigger problem that the situation precipitated into, could have been avoided. Now, neither the parents, nor anybody else in the family can trust the son for a long time. The mother has drawn on far more hurt and pain than what she would have dealt with at an earlier stage.

This is like **evading a drizzle, only to invite a storm**. In certain contexts, communication becomes time sensitive. No matter how unpleasant or uncomfortable it may seem, it has to be done when the time is right.

A team of software engineers is developing software for a certain client, when they hit a major technical roadblock which becomes a showstopper in advancing further. In such a scenario, even though informing the client that the work has come to an unexpected standstill is an unpleasant conversation, the project manager has to do it.

Never evade a drizzle at the cost of inviting a storm. The client may get upset and raise a hue and cry, but it is better to communicate at an early stage than to keep it in the dark for now and then deal with a bigger problem later. The client is going to assume that work is progressing and when the deadline arrives, a considerable time interval would have elapsed and the problem at hand would be far more critical. Hence, it is better to communicate sooner than later in such scenarios to avoid an implosion.

For the *disease* of miscommunication, timely information is the best *cure*. Know the disease to find how it can be prevented. All the reasons listed above would help us understand the various scenarios that are prone to miscommunication.

We should study our own communication to see if we are afflicted by any of the above symptoms. Spend some time to contemplate on this chapter and prepare an action-plan for steering clear of such miscommunication.

2

Becoming a Better Listener

Half the world's communication problems would be solved, if only people would realize the importance of listening and develop it. In this chapter, we shall discuss listening.

Firstly, we're not just interested in how we can become better listeners ourselves, but also in how those whom we are speaking with, can become better listeners as well. Secondly, listening well doesn't just mean listening well to the words that are being spoken. Listening goes well beyond the dimension of words, and to understand it fully, we will approach the topic in 3 steps.

Step 1 – Listen to the speaker, not your mind

In a classroom session, one of the students raised his hand to ask a question. When the professor nodded to him, he asked, "Professor, I've noticed that when I hear you or any of the other professors discuss a topic, I initially get the feeling that I've heard everything and understood it well. But sometimes, after the class is over, I realize I haven't understood it as thoroughly as I'd thought. Why does this happen?"

Many other students also raised their hands to suggest that they too had a similar experience. The professor smiled, "That's because when you're listening to me, you aren't only listening to me!"

"We're not? But you're the only one who's talking at that time! Who else could we be listening to?!" asked the intrigued students.

"To your mind." continued the professor, "While I'm talking, your mind is having a talk show of its own. It is constantly analyzing and dissecting what it hears... 'I know this,' 'I don't agree to this,' 'That is boring!', 'How could that be, I don't understand that,' 'That's easy!' Or the mind is focused elsewhere... 'I wonder what's for lunch today,' 'God... wish I could have a burger,' 'I need to checkout that new smartphone,' 'When will this class get over?!' etc.

"Let's take a quick test to see how well you listen," said the professor. "All you have to do is listen to a story and answer a question."

"Yes," said all the students in unison as they all sat upright, ready to listen.

"Once upon a time," began the professor, "there was a condominium of flats in a certain city. The condominium consisted of several ten and twelve storied buildings clustered together. Two particular buildings—one ten-storied and the other twelve-storied—stood right opposite each other. The ten-storied building was occupied by kindhearted and positive people. They would help each other, have merriments together, celebrate festivals together, and never indulge in fights or arguments with their neighbors.

"The people staying in the twelve-storied building were exactly the opposite. They were mean, selfish, shrewd and cunning. Many of them were alcoholics who would drink and get into brawls. The noise of fights and arguments would emanate from their building all the time, making the aura of the place very gloomy and depressing.

"One day, due to some reason, a fire started in some part of both the buildings. It was a breezy day and soon the fire spread in these buildings. Shortly afterwards, both the buildings were fiercely ablaze. Someone spotted the fire and cried out in fear. People started running helter-skelter in the commotion. Residents of the other buildings were afraid the fire might spread to their buildings as well. Someone cried out, 'There are nearly five-hundred people in the taller building and three-hundred in the other one. We need to put out the fire immediately. Call an ambulance!'

"Someone made the call and a few minutes later an ambulance rushed to the spot.

"'Quick... put the fire out... put the fire out...,' people cried.

"Some people were directing the ambulance to the twelve-storied building while some were directing it to the ten-storied building. An argument broke out between the people who had gathered downstairs as to which building should be saved first. 'The taller building first, it has got more people stuck in it,' said someone. 'No! The shorter building first!' said another."

Bringing his story to an end, the professor posed the question to his class. "Now tell me. Which fire should be put out first? Should they save the five-hundred people from the taller building first, or the three-hundred people from the other building?"

"The taller building has five-hundred people, while the shorter one has three-hundred. Naturally the building with the larger number of people has to be saved first," said one student.

"No... the three-hundred people in the shorter building are good people. It is more important to save three-hundred good people than five-hundred bad ones," said another student.

"Yes," almost everyone cried in unison, "Save the three-hundred good people!"

"The ambulance has reached the spot," the professor repeated his question, "Now which building's fire should be put out first?"

"The shorter one!" was the nearly unanimous reply.

The professor smiled, "My dear friends, *ambulances* don't put out fire... The *fire brigade* does! They have called an ambulance, not a fire brigade!"

Realizing their mistake, the students burst out laughing. They were so caught up in mulling over the question that they forgot about the difference between an ambulance and a fire brigade. In fact, they heard the mention of the ambulance and unconsciously assumed a fire brigade!

This example illustrates how our mind hears what it *wants* to hear instead of listening to what is actually being said. It is a deeply ingrained tendency of the mind to construct a story of its own while listening to what's being said and then get attached to this *concocted* version of the story, considering it to be authentic. We never realize when the mind has shifted our focus from what's really happening to the story being weaved within. It is only when our focus is pulled back to the what's really happening, like in the example above, that we realize the play of the mind.

We *feel* that we are listening to people when they talk, but this isn't always true. The mind is capable of functioning on a very subtle level and we never realize when it disrupts our focus. As soon as the speaker's words fall outside the bounds of the mind's logic and reasoning, it rejects them altogether. And that's not all. The biggest mistake follows; with the rejection of what others are saying, comes the complete disruption of our focus from the very act of listening. The mind diverts our focus from listening to something that it *wants* to think about or immediately gets into critically analyzing the words that it just rejected.

Analyzing and understanding words is not a bad thing, but it has to be done later, not *during* the conversation! But the mind would rather do it then and there. The conversation seems uninteresting or unimportant because the mind doesn't agree with what was said. This is how the mind vacillates and keeps us away from focusing on the conversation. The mind acts like a living entity, accompanying us in the conversation, deciding on our behalf, what we should listen to and what we shouldn't.

Imagine the mind to be a tool like a remote control. Ideally, we should be operating the remote control to decide which television channel to watch, but the way the mind encroaches, is like the remote control deciding which television channel we should or shouldn't watch!

This tendency is present in everyone to varying degrees. Its intensity varies in the same person depending on situations. When people are not able to concentrate on something, we hear them say, "I have a lot on my mind right now." During such times, their mind has created such a chaos within them, that they find it impossible to concentrate elsewhere.

How do we deal with this?

The sole, simple, and straight answer: By disciplining the mind.

With practice, we can learn to watch our thoughts with awareness and discipline them. With perseverance, we can stop the mind's dictating what we should say or do.

With regards to listening in a conversation, we have to first learn to identify when and how the mind tries to intervene and take things over. Then we have to direct it to remain silent while we listen. Interference is a deep tendency of the mind, so we cannot expect the mind to obediently remain silent the very first time we ask it to. It will try to rise back; it will try to speak; it will try to give you unsolicited advice; it will try to analyze the words it hears; it will try to label them, categorize them, judge them. If we get bored during the conversation, it will try to steal our focus and shift it to something else. It will try every tactic, but we have to be aware of all such attempts and identify them for what they are—interferences of the mind.

An enemy recognized is half-conquered; a problem understood is half-solved!

Once we become aware of the mind's interruptions, all we have to do is to interrupt it back, stop it, and shift our focus back to listening. The goal is to attain a no-mind state (one where the chattering mind is altogether absent) so that we may listen without any interruptions. This is the practice of meditation. As we get better at meditation, we will find our power of concentration has enhanced and our ability to listen has improved.

Step 2 – Empathetic listening

We have all been in conversations where we have felt that the listener is not paying attention to us. We are talking to someone and telling them something very crucial and important about ourselves. We feel that though this person is looking at us, they are not paying much attention. Their attention is unstable, their eyesight keeps drifting to things around us. Sometimes they're looking out of the window, sometimes at the ceiling, sometimes at the books on the table, they pick up their phone every time it rings and check even the most useless notifications. Their body language shows that they aren't really interested in listening to what we're saying.

Recall such a conversation and remember how you felt. Didn't you feel bad? Even if the person repeats to us all that we've said, we don't feel convinced that we've been fully heard. But why was the person not able to give us their undivided attention?

There could only be two reasons—either, what we were saying was not important to them, or *we* weren't important to them.

Needless to say, in either case we feel hurt. It is for this reason that listening shouldn't just be limited to hearing words. One has to go beyond words and connect with the feelings that the words are emanating from. This is known as *listening with empathy*. Empathize with the speaker; understand where they're coming from; sense what they are feeling as they utter those words. If we listen with complete attention, sincerity and sensitivity, we will be able to connect with the speaker at an experiential level, by feeling their emotions. This is the meaning of the well-known idiom *"stepping into someone's shoes."* Many a time, just listening with such sincerity solves or prevents several communication problems.

Morgan Scott Peck—an American psychiatrist and best-selling author—describes his experiences as a psychiatrist in one of his books. He says that in the first few counselling sessions, he would only listen to his patients' problems attentively and empathetically. Before he could even begin his treatment, 25% of his patients would already start feeling much better, thanks to his empathetic listening skill. He further writes, even simply listening to someone attentively and empathetically acts as an effective therapy for the speaker.

When it comes to relations, the ability to listen assumes far more importance, especially with married couples. From the youngest kid to the eldest grandparent, everyone wants to be heard. And yet it is the single most common complaint every family member has with nearly every other family member—that they are not heard! It is a common problem among married couples as well. Everyone has a perspective, and everyone wants theirs to be accepted.

Consider the example of a married couple. In spite of knowing that his perspective is different from his wife's, no special effort is made by the husband to understand her perspective. He just pretends to listen to her, but what he is really looking for is a chance for her to take a moment to breathe and he pounces at the opportunity to interrupt and begin speaking. This has a dual effect. One, because the wife is not given a proper chance to speak and be heard, it leaves her with a lingering feeling of injustice and unimportance. Two, because she is feeling what she is, she in turn doesn't want to listen to what her husband says either. The same could very well be applicable to the wife, or in fact anyone in a personal or professional relationship.

At the workplace too, the ability to listen is of paramount importance in connecting with every team member. Each one would surely have their own perspective and hearing them out, is crucial to maintain a healthy work environment. When team members feel that they have been heard, it gives them a sense of closure, of completion. They feel wanted, important; they feel that their opinion matters. This encourages them to work harder and better. Only when they have been heard, do they open up to others' perspectives as well. Otherwise, they find it difficult to listen to others.

To make this work, the one and only way is to make an honest effort to hear them out. In a professional environment, here are some tips we can follow to ensure that we listen well and also make the person feel that they have been properly heard (for that is equally important!).

- After you hear them out, summarize what you have understood to them. This way, you will not only get a chance to confirm the correctness of what you've understood, but also give the other person a sense of assurance that you have heard them attentively.

- You can ask them relevant, contextual, and genuine questions to make them feel that you're attentive. However, such questions should not be posed by interrupting them, but after they have said what they wanted to or when they are prepared to take questions or responses.

- Maintain steady eye contact and keep nodding your head (not too rigorously) to show them that you are present 100% and listening.

- Despite attentively listening, if the speaker poses a question or makes a comment that you're unable to respond to, you can honestly tell them that you were busy listening to them and cannot respond to their question or comment at that moment and that you will get back to them about it later.

With constant study and practice, one can master this skill of empathetic listening. When we understand a topic well and practice it regularly with awareness, the skill begins to evolve. Let us take another step towards studying the art of listening, so as to hone this skill.

Step 3 – Keeping your listeners' attention engaged

Good listening skill is a sign of a trained and disciplined mind, however, not everyone in the world possesses it. Communicating with people who are not good at listening becomes a grave and frustrating challenge. In such cases, the responsibility of carrying out a sustained conversation falls on the shoulders of those who are good at it.

An untrained mind is very fickle, restless, and constantly wanders like a butterfly. It instantly loses interest in any conversation that it finds boring. However, if something in the conversation grabs its attention, it is capable of remarkable concentration as well. One can grab people's attention effectively by saying something that captures their imagination, arouses their curiosity, or fires their ambition.

However important or impressive the content of our speech may be, if we cannot grab the attention of our audience and sustain it, we will never be able to communicate with them. Hence, the art of engaging people's attention is a crucial skill for effective communication. Let us look at some ways to achieve this.

Speak Enthusiastically - When speaking to the audience, speak with enthusiasm, energy, and a spark. Back in school or college days, which teacher's class did we love attending? Those who spoke energetically, or those who spoke lethargically? However knowledgeable a teacher may be, if they do not present their content enthusiastically, they will never be able to hold the attention of their class. The same applies to any conversation we have. If we want to make sure we grab and hold our listeners' attention, one way to do that is to speak enthusiastically.

But how can one muster the energy and enthusiasm just like that? The answer is: act-as-if. "Act-as-if" is a technique where we imagine that we are already feeling the emotion that we wish to arouse, and then start acting out the emotion. In this case, we act as if we are already feeling extremely enthusiastic. The wonderful thing about this technique is that soon, we actually start feeling enthusiastic and full of energy! What a beautiful phenomenon, isn't it?! You can also use this technique in many other situations of life as well.

Modulate your Voice – Imagine that you are trying to communicate something in an environment that is already noisy and chaotic. People are arguing around you, their attention is scattered, and no one is in the frame to listen. At such times, if you add to the chaos by speaking in a raised voice yourself, no one will hear you because the air is already full of loud voices.

At such times, we can draw people's attention by using hand gestures or conscious body language, and then start speaking in a lower than normal voice. They will see that you are talking but they won't be able to hear you. This will get them to settle down and even make the others settle down because they want to hear what you are saying. In this way, you can achieve two goals: the atmosphere calms down and you're able to get your speech through to your audience.

Use Engaging Phrases – Another way to make sure your audience is ready and listening before you get to the point, is to begin by using engaging phrases. Some examples are:

- There is something very important I want to tell you…
- There is something very interesting I have been thinking of sharing with you, I'm sure you'll love this…
- You may find this very odd or amusing but…
- I could have told you this earlier, but I thought I'd better wait for the right time, which is now…
- Please give me all your attention, because we are both going to need this…

Such beginnings entice the interest of a listener and they get into a listening mode to hear what you have to say.

Interact with the audience – Long monologues make the attention of your listeners sway to other things at some point. Hence, if you're sure that your speech is going to be a long one, make sure you include elements like Q&A's or take opinions from your audience. You may even ask them questions. With this, you ensure that your audience feels involved and they are kept on their toes.

All these techniques are applicable to both public speaking as well as private conversations. These techniques will help you draw (and keep) your listener's attention, making sure they hear you well.

3

Using the Right Words

In the process of developing our communication skills, we get the opportunity to closely observe and study the communication style of a lot of people. Based on their communication style, there are broadly three categories of people:

1. Those who mostly use positive, encouraging, and affirmative words whenever they speak.

2. Those whose choice of words depends on the situation or mood they're in. Their choice could be positive or negative, sarcastic or sincere, based on how they are feeling within.

3. Those who mostly speak negative words and hence evidently feel negative emotions most of the time.

Let's understand how conversing with people from each of these categories affects us.

Imagine you have a businessman-friend who belongs to the third category. All the time, he talks about how the business is poor, how the global economy is heading towards a decline, how the government is looting him by levying heavy taxes, how people are thugs waiting for an opportunity to strip him of his money.

How would you feel while conversing with such a person? Sad and depressed, right? As if all hope has been sucked out of life! Would anyone want to meet such a person the second time? Would we ever think of calling him up to spend a day together? Never!

Now imagine a person of the second category. You have met your friend after many years, sitting in a café and fondly bringing each other up to date on your lives. Your friend is happy to have met you and is speaking in a pleasant manner using positive words. Suddenly, he receives a phone call, and his body language and facial expression change. His conversation begins to agitate him. He starts speaking negative words and abusing the other person over the phone.

After disconnecting the call, he continues to be in a bad mood and his words and demeanor are acutely negative and critical. Would you feel comfortable in his company? When he is in high spirits, things will be okay, but once his mood changes, speaking to him would be an unpleasant experience!

Few indeed are those, who belong to the first category. These people have trained themselves to always choose positive words. Speaking to them is always a pleasure, although one may not know why one loves talking to them. They love the positive and uplifting feeling they derive by conversing with these people.

Our vocabulary is greatly influenced by our upbringing and general surroundings. A decent and educated person would mostly employ a courteous and respectful vocabulary. On the other hand, one who has been surrounded by people who use unrefined and abusive language will soon adopt the same style. This isn't always deliberate; it happens naturally. We tend to unconsciously soak in and learn from our surroundings.

However, if we want to rise above our surroundings to master the art of communication, we need to consciously train ourselves to new habits. We have to learn to filter out negative words from our vocabulary and develop a new vocabulary to be able to say negative things in a positive way. It is understandable that not every statement we speak, can be positive; there could be negative aspects that we will have to communicate. But if we learn the skill of presenting them with the help of positive and affirmative words, it will be a great leap forward in learning not only to be a good communicator but also a positive person.

A ten-year old girl makes a painting and excitedly shows it to her father. Her father is busy working on his laptop and is annoyed at this interruption. He unwillingly takes the painting in his hands and comments on it in the following words:

"Is that a border line you've drawn around all the objects? It's so uneven, too thick at some places and too thin otherwise. And why are you adding so much water to the colors? The colors look so faded! The human figures look like they are half-dead! Draw them better. I can see smudges of your finger and palm all over the painting. Why don't you clean your hands while painting?!"

Such a feedback will probably discourage the little girl from painting again, perhaps forever!

What if he were to give his feedback as follows?

"Fantastic! I love your idea of drawing a black border around the objects; it makes them stand out nicely; just that if you could make the line more even, it will look even more beautiful! The amount of water you are adding to your colors is making them look faint. If you add less water, you'll get a better color after the paint dries. Your technique of adding more water works perfectly for painting the sky, as it needs to look faint blue. I'm glad you have drawn human figures too. I am sure with time and practice you will draw even better figures with finer details. And yes... one little tip for you, since you have done such a fantastic job with your first painting – keep washing your hands clean every now and then, so that you don't get finger and palm smudges on your drawing page. Awesome painting... I love it! Keep it up!"

In the second instance, the feedback is worded such that the criticism is conveyed in a positive manner along with appreciation. Both the feedbacks will have contrasting effects on the girl. While the former will make her feel dejected and discouraged, the latter will make her feel good and will encourage her to improve herself.

Don't criticize, but critiguide! *Critiguiding* is a new term that you won't find in the dictionary. It stands for constructive criticism, done with the intention of encouragement and improvement. Having positive communication doesn't mean one has to only say positive things and never criticize. Constructive criticism is important for growth, but it has to be communicated properly. We will discuss this in more depth in a later chapter.

A person is lying on a hospital bed, looking pale and scrawny as his relatives and friends visit him. One of them says, "You look so weak. As soon as you are discharged, you should eat well and put on some weight, so that you don't look like someone who's spent two weeks in bed."

A little later another relative comes by and says, "Congratulations! You get to go home today! As soon as you are back home, you're going to do everything you can to get back to your healthy self!"

Notice the difference in the way both these relatives chose their words to communicate the same thing. Patients are in an especially vulnerable state of mind and they need all the good wishes and positivity they can get. In such cases, a relative who speaks positively seems a far more desirable company than someone who is negative.

People, who inadvertently choose negative words, develop a negative aura around them over a period of time. Even before they open their mouth to speak, people feel an unexplained urge to either not speak to them at all or to keep the conversation as short as possible. On the other hand, those who choose positive words, build a positive aura around them. People love speaking to them for hours. Even if someone approaches them with a specific agenda, they end up conversing with them for hours, because it is a pleasant experience. Wouldn't it be nice to be such a person?!

There is another sub-category of people, who do not use as many negative words as those belonging to the third category described above. But their choice of words illustrates their lackluster and damp attitude towards everything. If you greet them, "Hello! How are you doing?", their most likely monosyllabic reply would be, "Okay" or "Fine" with an expressionless face. If you excitedly forward a useful or inspirational message to them, they will reply, "I know," "I've read this," or "I've heard this before." You may feel "That's it?! Is that all you've got to say?!" In short, not only are they devoid of energy; they also make others feel the same too! Such people never speak words of appreciation. After conversing with them, we're invariably left with a sentiment that mirrors their outlook, "Life is boring and there's absolutely nothing to be gained from being too passionate about anything." Such people may not be termed "negative" per se, but they aren't very positive either!

The purpose of studying these categories of people and their characteristics is also meant for us to do some soul-searching within ourselves. We need to introspect and find out which category *we* fall into.

- Which words do I use in my daily communication?
- What do people feel when they communicate with me?
- Do I fall in the broad category of a negative person? If I do, I need to start working on my communication.

As you develop the habit of using positive and affirmative words, you will notice a magical change in your communication.

Let us consider another very well-known example of the magic that positive words bring to communication.

A beggar would stand outside the entrance to a church every Sunday, with his hat in his hands, begging for alms. He had kept a signboard made from a torn cardboard box next to him on the street. The board said, "I am blind. Please help me!" Several churchgoers would pass by him every Sunday, but he wouldn't receive much alms.

One day, a young boy happened to read the blind beggar's signboard. He picked up the board, wrote something on it, and kept it back.

The blind beggar could sense that someone had written something on his board. To his amazement, he suddenly started hearing the jingle of coins falling into his hat – not one or two, but several. Soon his hat was too heavy to be held in one hand and the blind man blessed the young boy.

The young boy had scratched the words on the board and written, "It's a beautiful day today! I can't see it but blessed are those who can!"

In both the cases, the message on the board communicated that the beggar was blind, but the way they communicated it was starkly different. The first message had a sad undertone, carrying the sentiment that the world is full of sorrow and poverty. People tend to ignore things that make them feel depressed. And so, the churchgoers would ignore the beggar. However, the second message told them how beautiful the world is and how lucky they were. A mere alteration of words changed their response.

This is the magic of positive words! The words we use have a profound effect on the emotions we feel. Positive words arouse positive feelings, while negative words trigger negative feelings.

Let's try a little experiment. Repeat the words, "O God, bless the world, bless everyone!" But while you do that, try to arouse the feeling of anger or hatred in yourself. Feel the emotion and keep repeating the words.

Not very easy, isn't it?! It is almost impossible to link a negative feeling with positive words. Now try the same while repeating something negative, and you will see that the feeling rises exponentially till it fills you up completely. And it wasn't very hard either! This means, on a subconscious level, positive words are linked with positive feelings and negative words are linked with negative feelings. The more positive words we use, the faster and stronger the feelings associated with them naturally and effortlessly grow within us.

If someone were to tell us, "Try and feel the positivity rise in you and sense the energy," we might find it a little hard to do. But the use of positive words makes the same thing happen easily and naturally. This is particularly important in communication because even if our listener misses a word here or there, he will often succeed in sensing our emotions. Hence, it is important to build a strong vocabulary of positive, encouraging, and pleasing words.

So how do we go about doing that? What's the action plan to build the right vocabulary?

Step 1 – Get rid of the excessively negative words, especially abusive words from your vocabulary. Suppose you were asked to write any abusive word that you commonly use on a piece of paper and then made to sign on it. What if this paper, signed by you, were to be framed and displayed to all those whom you love and respect, like your parents, teachers, spouse, mentor, etc.? Would you sign on it? Would you confess that you utter such words? If you won't, then do such words that you even refuse to take responsibility for, deserve to be in your vocabulary?

Step 2 – Monitor your words all day, and list down all the negative words you speak. Make a note also of the insipid, dull, and bland words. At the end of the day, review this list and replace them with positive words. Resolve to repeat the sentences from the day before, with the replaced words. With this exercise, you will notice that your communication style is becoming increasingly positive and people will enjoy speaking to you. You will also notice their pleasure!

Use words like "Thank you," "Please," "Pardon me," "My apologies" unsparingly. These words illustrate the qualities of humility, courtesy, self-control, simplicity, sincerity, respect, and conviction. Using them at the right time in the right way, will further enhance your communication, making it even more pleasant.

Step 3 – Add new words to your vocabulary. Always make note of new positive words, phrases and idioms, so as to use them in your speech. Search for the meaning of new words, understand their context and keep them ready for later use. Make it a practice to experiment with daily sentences by trying to frame them little differently. For example, instead of greeting people with a regular

"Good morning", you may say "Best of the mornings to you!" and notice the smile on their faces! Your listeners will look forward to seeing you and talking to you.

Having understood the importance of words in the art of communication, we will now move to the next stage to understand the importance of gentleness in speech.

4
Gentleness in Speech

After working on becoming a better listener and building a positive vocabulary, the next stage is to adopt a gentle and sweet manner of speaking.

Speaking the right words in the right way, not only solves but also prevents several problems. People tend to like us and want to speak to us. Anyone, who is in the habit of speaking gently using positive words, leads a happy, peaceful, and harmonious life. We have already seen how words can affect our emotions and our life. Let us now look at how the way we speak profoundly affects our mind and body.

The importance of using a gentle language and demeanor is not a recent discovery but has been reinforced since ages. Over the years, several poets, writers, thinkers, and communication experts have professed it. A language that treats everyone with love, respect, and humility, instantly pleases people.

Let us understand this with an example. Put yourself in the shoes of a customer support representative, who attends to phone calls from consumers. They often receive phone calls from irate customers, who speak rudely, at times, abusively.

Recall any conversation in which you had an argument, were scolded, or abused. What were the bodily sensations you felt at that moment? Your heart rate would have quickened. Your blood pressure would have plummeted. Your forehead and palms would have become sweaty. Your breath would have become rapid and shallow. Your chest would have perhaps tightened.

The same thing happens when you talk to an angry and frustrated customer on the phone. You have to take great effort to maintain your calm and respond to the customer. Besides, speaking to such a person makes you feel low, sapping your energy, and affecting your performance for the rest of the day.

As against that, imagine talking to a pleasant and courteous customer. For someone who attends hundreds of calls a day, it would be such a relief to come across a gentle and pleasant voice!

Now that we know the effect it has on us, it becomes our responsibility to make sure that others do not suffer because of our speech. Hence, our speech has to be gentle and soothing. Even if we are stern or strict, we should still choose gentle ways and respectful language.

Consider a little boy, who has made a mistake and has to face his father. Or an employee, who has goofed up and has been summoned by his boss. The father or the boss can either be loud, rude, and insulting while reprimanding, or choose to use a respectful and gentle manner of speaking, even while being stern. Which kind of conversation do you think will help the son or the employee to refrain from repeating the mistake?

"I do understand that mistakes happen, and they are not always done purposely. I don't want you to worry about this instance. I trust you and your conscience. I'm sure that you're capable of easily getting over this mistake and ensuring that it doesn't repeat."

By choosing the right words and manner of speaking, not only do they convey their message correctly but also make sure that the listener does not endure any pain. Having been treated with respect despite committing the mistake, both the son and the employee will be more committed towards their father or boss.

Following are some example phrases that can help make your communication gentle and empathetic:

"I trust you" – Sometimes, we may have justified reasons to distrust someone, but we can choose not to. By trusting people against our judgement, we may not have much to lose, but a lot to gain. We boost their morale and inspire them to become better versions of themselves. In professional relationships, trust strengthens the bonds of sincerity and dedication.

"I can understand you" – Everyone wants to be heard and understood. Hence, it is helpful to actually say it in words. It goes a long way in making your listener feel calm and relieved.

- I can understand where you're coming from.
- I can fully understand how you're feeling right now.

"You are right" – This is a magical phrase that everyone wants to hear. Everyone thinks they are right, and they are never tired of hearing it! When we tell someone that they are right, the sense of completion and acceptance makes them feel good. Following are some examples of how we can use this phrase even while disagreeing with someone:

- You are right in your way, but we have to go by rules.
- What you say is perfectly right, but you should say the same thing calmly.
- You are right in your place, but you also need to understand where he is coming from. What he says is right from his perspective.
- Your suggestion is excellent, but I don't think it would be much effective in this context.

"I am with you" – Nothing assures people of your empathy more than telling them, "I am with you." This gives them a sense of security. They can be assured that there is someone they can rely on, no matter what. These words do wonders by bolstering their courage and making them feel a fresh wave of energy and resolve.

These examples can help you develop a likeable manner of speaking. Regardless of the language, everyone likes a pleasant conversation. Professionals are especially trained to speak cordially and respectfully at work. Customer care executives undergo rigorous training to develop a polite and courteous way of speaking to customers.

Adopting such methods of communication at work helps create a better work environment and develop camaraderie with colleagues. At home and with friends, speaking with everyone gently, sweetly, and positively, strengthens relationships and fosters respect.

5

Expressing that You Care

"People don't care how much you know, until they know how much you care," said Theodore Roosevelt, the 36th president of the United States of America.

We could probably make a small addition to the quote to make its meaning a little more explicit, "People don't care how much you know, until they know how much you care... *about them*." This little addition specifies the intent beyond the general caring of a topic, a situation, or a company. It makes it specific for a person or group.

If you've ever been at the receiving end of a one-sided conversation, you would have probably felt that the other person didn't care about you. They cared more about speaking about themselves. No matter what topic you bring up, instead of listening and asking questions, they try to talk about a similar situation in their own life. They try to center the discussion on their own story.

This is fine when the person is quoting his examples to sincerely guide us.

In any conversation, we should give due importance to the other person. So, the next time you're in a meeting or on a call, besides committing to listen, also ask questions, be curious enough to show that you really care about the other person. By doing this, you will demonstrate a sense of sincerity.

But does this mean we should abandon the topic at hand, and just talk about the other person?

Of course, not! Imagine that you are an investment consultant and are trying to explain a profitable investment option to your client. Now, it is not that you should keep aside the investment option and only talk about your client–his likes, dislikes, and his life. No, that would be pleasing to your client to a certain extent (as long as you're not overdoing it!) but counterproductive. The point is to genuinely care for the client and also express it in your words to make him feel that you care about him and that everything you are talking about is actually for his betterment.

Example 1:

"Sir, let me explain to you this investment option that you will find very lucrative. I can assure you that investing in this will be the best decision you make today."

Example 2:

"Sir, the moment I was briefed by my company about this investment option, the first person I thought of was you. Since then, I've been very excited to share this with you. So, thank you so much for giving me the opportunity."

The second example clearly demonstrates your genuine care for your client. Although both the statements are conveying the same thing, the second one has a better chance of pleasing him and making him attentive to what you are about to say. People like it when we make them the center of the conversation.

Suppose you summon a waiter in a restaurant to place your order, "I'll have a sandwich and a cup of coffee."

"We have three kinds of sandwiches in the menu. Which one shall I get?" he asks.

Now the waiter could have replied differently:

"We are serving three different kinds of sandwiches for you today. Which one would you like to enjoy?"

The difference is subtle but quite evident. The second instance clearly shows that the waiter is polite and considerate. The conversation will be pleasant.

Understand this with another example: Imagine that you take a little help from your colleagues to complete a particular project successfully. Later, when you are being appreciated for your work in the presence of the entire team, you say, "It wasn't just me. I had my friends working with me on it. It was us!" In spite of having done most of the project work yourself, you remember to share the credit with your colleagues instead of hogging it yourself.

By rising above the "I" to include the "we", you show that you are not self-centered and do care about others. Words like "I, me, mine" convey one's self-centeredness and egotism. So, use them as sparingly as you can so that you don't sound like you care only about yourself.

Let us now understand the right use of the words "I" and "you". There are situations where we need to replace one with the other.

For example, when pointing out someone's mistake, instead of saying, "**You** need to be more careful while doing such a critical task," you can say, "**I** would be more careful while doing such a critical task," or "**We** need to be more careful while doing such tasks."

Using "I" or "we" instead of "you" in such cases, makes your statements less accusatory and at the same time conveys your point. Your feedback is delivered gently. Remember that driving the point home and getting the desired result is more important. So, if the mistake is grave and you want to make sure that it is not repeated, you can be firm when you say the same words. With this, the seriousness of the situation gets communicated without affecting the work environment negatively.

Even while conversing with family members, using accusatory sentences could result in strained relationships and a bad mood at home. Explain to them their mistakes in the language of "I", "we", or "us", so that they would want to listen to you and get motivated to better themselves.

PART 2
DEEPER NUANCES OF COMMUNICATION

Speech is silver, but silence is golden.

Those who agree with this quote, have realized the importance of silence. There are two interpretations of the word "silence."

The first interpretation refers to the obvious meaning of silence, which is when you choose not to speak about something. Thus, it is silence in the literal sense. It refers to situations where talking too much becomes harmful to the speaker. It either gets him into trouble or spoils his reputation. So, when viewed from this perspective, the quote basically underlines the importance of knowing when to talk and when to remain silent.

The other interpretation is a subtler one that usually evades many of us. This silence refers to inner silence—the silence of the mind. Our mind is continuously chattering. It constantly engages in comparing, judging, and labelling things. It is this mind that keeps us from feeling calm.

Silencing this noisy faculty of the mind is one of the primary goals of spiritual growth. And how is it done? With meditation. If the judgmental mind is the disease, then meditation is the surefire cure.

If we study the lives of all the prominent and successful people in any era, we will find that nearly all of them had the habit of meditation. Meditation is the way to silence the mind and connect to one's true self.

When we practice meditation, our mind becomes quiet and a peaceful stillness ensues. When whatever we do—be it our daily tasks or communication—stems from inner silence, it naturally leads to the best result.

Imagine working on a laptop that has very low memory and very slow processing power. How sluggish and inefficient it would be to work with it! And then imagine a state-of-the-art laptop with the latest specs. Working on it would not just be efficient but also pleasant. So it is with meditation. Meditation helps us unleash our latent potential, making it possible to achieve extraordinary results.

With the practice of meditation, our level of awareness rises, and when our communication emerges from such a heightened level of awareness, it comes out perfectly. The right words, the right feelings, empathy, positivity—all make our communication successful, beneficial, and pleasant for us and also those around us.

6

Appreciating and Complimenting

Seeking appreciation is a human tendency. By appreciating others, we not only make them feel good about themselves but also enrich our life. Even a few words of appreciation for their good deeds can uplift their mood, motivate them to do better, and give us a sense of satisfaction.

There is a fine line between authentic appreciation and flattery. One has to understand the other's strengths and then choose the right words in the right way at the right time to appreciate them.

Like the art of listening, appreciating someone and complementing them is also a subtle art. Not everyone is naturally capable of it. Many people hesitate to appreciate others and justify against giving compliments: "This is how I am!" or "Too much appreciation goes to peoples' heads. Now we don't want that, do we?!" or even "Is appreciation really necessary? He's just doing his job, right?"

Failing to appreciate or compliment someone at the right time is like a missed opportunity. One little sentence, a couple of words that hardly costs you more than a few seconds and a little energy, but to what result? The listener is motivated to get better at what they were appreciated about. It boosts their confidence and also improves your relationship with them.

Appreciating someone is an art because, like any other art, it has its subtleties that one has to grasp with constant study and practice. One cannot use a standard appreciation template for everyone. Each person has to be appreciated differently for their uniqueness. So, one has to keep creatively inventing.

For example, you won't compliment your boss the same way as you would a subordinate or a colleague. To appreciate a colleague you would say, "I'm happy to see your sincerity at work," or "It would be great if everyone could be as committed as you are," or "I appreciate your team spirit!" or "The way you handled this project in this challenging phase is commendable!"

When you are complimenting your boss, you will need to be more careful. Your choice of words would be completely different. To your boss, you are more likely to say something like, "Your dedication to your work is really inspiring! We all get to learn a lot from you!"

At home, the way you appreciate little kids wouldn't be the way you would appreciate teenagers or grown-ups. To learn this art, you have to observe people and study them. You may even have to experiment a little to find out what works with whom. Depending on the situation, you may have to appreciate someone in isolation or in a group, some directly or some indirectly through someone else.

In the case of children, appreciating them directly works far better than indirectly saying appreciative words about them to others in their presence.

Sometimes it works best to appreciate someone in front of those whom he or she regards highly. For example, when a husband appreciates his wife in the presence of her parents, it will gladden her.

All these ways have to be explored and used at different times with different people. Specific ways work with specific people and situations. We need to keep experimenting to learn and get better at this. We may hesitate in the beginning as we consciously develop this habit, especially if we haven't been in the habit of appreciating frequently. But as time goes by and our practice goes deeper and wider, we will grow comfortable and the habit will become natural and effortless.

Appreciation and compliments are especially important in the case of children. It makes them feel confident. Children look up to their parents and teachers. When they are adequately appreciated by them, they tend to have stronger confidence and a better self-image. In their formative years, such appreciation forges their personality and pushes them to develop the qualities they are appreciated for.

For example, if a child cracks a joke or does something funny and notices that everyone is laughing, he feels encouraged to experiment with humor. Hence, it is important that parents observe their children very closely and verbalize their appreciation in the right manner and magnitude. Instead of resorting to over-enthusiastic appreciation and flattery less frequently, give small bits of genuine appreciation more frequently. Some examples: "Congratulations! You worked really hard for this," "You should be proud of yourself!" "That's a very creative answer!" or "Your unique answer nailed that question!"

When we compliment people, it gives them a sense of approval and makes them feel special. They too get to know us better. They are assured that we are their well-wishers; that we are genuinely interested in their growth and happy about their accomplishments. This assurance has a profoundly positive effect on our relationship with them. But the key word here is "genuinely."

The sentiment behind appreciating others has to be genuine. People can easily sense when appreciation is faked. By indulging in fake appreciation, we could do ourselves more harm than good. We might imagine that we have successfully faked sincerity and made others believe it. But in the longer run, we will be known as a fake and insincere person. We will lose our worthiness and our words will lose credibility.

With children too, if our words of appreciation are not sincere, they won't really feel encouraged. Children are extremely perceptive in such matters. Effusive or overly general encouragement may also be perceived as insincerity. Hence, we should always keep a check on the authenticity of our feelings while appreciating others.

To consciously develop the habit of genuinely appreciating and complimenting others, let us understand the three kinds of appreciation:

1. **Appreciating people for their work** – Being appreciated for their work is important and necessary for most people. Such appreciation—even in a few words—encourages them to do even better and enhances their perseverance. "Well done", "Good job" or "You're smart" are common encouraging words for tasks that are well done, provided they are backed by genuine feelings.

2. **Appreciating people for their qualities** – When we appreciate people for their qualities such as creativity, empathy, flexibility, forgiveness, kindness, or patience, they begin to identify themselves with those qualities. If someone is repeatedly appreciated for being kind, he begins to develop that quality within him. The next time he is in a situation where he can act kindly, he is encouraged to do so with extra zeal. Hence, we should appreciate even the smallest demonstration of a good quality, so that it grows.

   Looking for virtues in people also helps us look at them in positive light. For some reason, if we are unable to appreciate certain people for their work, we can appreciate them for their qualities as the next best alternative.

3. **Appreciating people for their possessions** – Appreciating people for their possessions is yet another way. Here are some examples: "That's a fantastic tie you're wearing today. It suits your personality!" "Your house is so beautiful! It's so spacious, airy, and bright." With children: "I love what you've done with your study table. Those little stars brighten up the place!" "I'm happy about the way you've kept your bicycle clean and in perfect working condition."

Finally, it helps to keep a daily scorecard to develop the habit of appreciation. Every day, express your appreciation for individuals you know intimately, as well as for strangers that you come across. Experiment with the different forms of appreciation described earlier. Observe how deeply people receive your appreciation when you find the right way to deliver it. Set a daily goal of appreciating at least ten people. Resolve not to end your day without achieving your daily quota. Appreciate your spouse, children, parents, friends, staff or colleagues. Do this every day for six months until it becomes your second nature.

As we develop the habit of appreciation, it helps to expand the circle of people whom we appreciate. Our society flourishes because of connections. We cannot survive without other people. Nobody grows their own food, packs it, and trucks it into their own town. Many people contribute to make it happen. The food we eat probably has more than thirty to forty people involved in it before it gets to our table. Although they may be strangers, the people who serve us by doing their part in making our life function, deserve our thanks and appreciation too!

7

Caring about Others' Self-image

There are two facets to our personality—two images so to say. One is the external image or the outwardly projected image, while the other is the inner image or the self-image.

The external image is the way we want the world to know us. When people interact with us, this is how we wish them to receive us. Naturally everyone wants to be perceived as a good person, so they make efforts to maintain a good projected image.

On the other hand, the self-image is how we perceive ourselves within; the image we have held about ourselves. It is about how we look at ourselves at a deeper level. It is how we feel about ourselves when we see when we look in the mirror.

The self-image is a collective of numerous self-impressions that have been built over time within us. These self-impressions are usually positive. Every person tends to think of himself as righteous and honorable. If one was to speak to criminals who were convicted, they will try to justify how they were right in doing what they did.

Our self-image can be positive, boosting our confidence about the way we feel and act. It could also be negative, making us doubt our capabilities and ideas. There are many attributes that keep getting added to our self-image, such as "intelligent," "kind," "generous," "strong," "righteous." Consequently, we identify ourselves with our self-image.

Our self-image becomes the basis for our existence. When someone speaks in such a way as to attack our self-image, we subconsciously perceive it as an attack on ourselves. It is as if someone is attacking our mirror image but we perceive it as an attack on our real self. There are three ways we can react.

1. Accept the speaker's statements and change one's self-image. This requires a a willingness to introspect and flexibility to change oneself. But this is rarely the case, mainly because one's ego comes in the way. So, unless the words are coming from someone the person adores and considers as an idol or mentor, one will not agree to change his self-image.

2. Assume a fiercely defensive stance and prove the speaker wrong. The rigid mind resists change by thinking, "I'm perfect the way I am; why should I change for them?!" Hence, the listener tries to retaliate and reject what is being said.

3. Say nothing but harbor the feeling of hatred for the speaker. This happens in cases where the listener is unable to argue or retaliate (like in the case of an employee and his boss).

If we use harsh words that hurt the listener's self-image, it could lead to serious miscommunication. Unless the listener is genuinely convinced about changing his self-image, he is bound to give the second or third kind of reaction. Hence, it is important to learn how to communicate in such a way as to not hurt others' self-image.

There are different words that hurt different people in different ways. With careful attention and study, we can find out which words need to be replaced so as to make sure no one feels hurt.

Let us understand this with the example of the communication between a father and son. The father has just found that his son has fallen into bad company and has taken up to smoking. To rebuff his son, the father says, "How many times have I told you not to hang out with those good-for-nothing friends of yours?! You're becoming one yourself! And now you have hit a new low... Smoking! Very soon, you will be acting and speaking like those tramps. You're an embarrassment to the whole family. If you care even a little bit about your family, you will drop this dirty habit and your filthy company too!"

By speaking this way, the father attacks his son's self-image and hurts his ego. Even if the son knows that he is wrong, he will continue on this path of self-sabotage purely out of spite and cause himself physical and mental distress. He will perceive himself as a good and justified person and his father, the wrong one. The two possible ways the son may react (as discussed above) are:

He may get defensive and argue with his father, justifying how his friends are good and how they always support one another. The argument may even lead to heated words and the father and son may grow further apart. If the father continues to criticize him this way, the situation may get even more critical and the son may take extreme measures that will be disastrous for himself and his family.

Alternately, if the son is too timid to argue with his father, he won't say anything, but will silently hate his father. This will create a rift between them, which can perhaps last for a lifetime, unless one of them decides to work on it.

This is not just miscommunication; this is a complete breakdown of communication.

Now, if the father wants to motivate his son to alter his habits without hurting his self-image, he will need to adopt a different approach. He will deal with his son based on the understanding that **it is the person's habits that are wrong; not the person himself.** Someone who lies is basically a good person but with the bad habit of lying. Someone who smokes or drinks, is basically a good person with the bad affliction of smoking or drinking. Let us see how the conversation would go, had the father spoken to his son with this understanding.

"My dear son, it has come to my notice that you've fallen into bad company and have taken up smoking. I know that you are a good person at heart, but you need to understand how bad this habit is. You may have taken up smoking because of peer pressure, which also brings me to the point of how important one's company is. I proudly believe that you are capable of doing much better in life. You only have to make some little changes.

"Your friends are not bad people either. I appreciate the camaraderie that all of you share. But certain habits they have grown with are not healthy. They need to be woken up to this realization. If you can help them, that would be great. If not, the least you can do is to distance yourself from them so that you may grow out of such habits. Don't you feel that's the best thing to do?"

In this conversation, the father is able to convey his concerns to his son without belittling him and attacking his self-image. He reassures his son that even after all that he has done, he believes in his capabilities and is proud of him. Such a conversation has a better chance of finding his son in a listening mode and being more receptive to his words.

Mostly, conversations escalate when one tries to point out the other's mistakes. If we keep in mind that it isn't the person who is wrong but his habits or situational reaction, the conversation will be amicable and pleasant to both the parties.

Many saints and philosophers have repeatedly said, "There are no bad people; just good people with bad habits. Do not identify yourself with your vices. You and your vices are not one. It is entirely possible to separate yourself from your vices and get rid of them."

With this understanding, incorporate the following phrases in your communication so that you do not attack the other's self-image:

- I am not saying you are a bad person, it's just that I think you shouldn't have done this one thing.
- You are a good person, but your addiction is holding you back from being your best.

- Success is within your grasp; you just have to change this one thing.

- I'm not saying you are careless, but this task is too critical. So even a small mistake can have grave effects. You just need to be more attentive and that should do it.

In this way, when we speak to people by separating them from their vices or mistakes, not only do we convey our words without attacking their self-image, but also show trust in their ability to improve themselves. We are able to highlight their negativities in a positive language and give them direction, motivation, and confidence to get better.

Sometimes, we may hurt the other person's self-image inadvertently. In such cases, we have to take preventive measures to avoid such situations in the first place. Let us consider another example to understand this.

Rakesh was Firoz's boss. They both conducted internal audits in their company. Rakesh frequently requested Firoz for spreadsheet reports. Firoz wasn't particularly good at creating macros to automate data processing, required for preparing these reports. Consequently, his reports would always have errors—some so critical that they would end up in huge miscalculations. Rakesh wanted to discuss this with Firoz but kept holding himself back, worried that Firoz might take his feedback negatively.

One day, Rakesh was already having a bad workday and Firoz sent him yet another report with such an error. In a fit of rage, Rakesh barged out of his cabin, stomped to Firoz's cubicle, and roared, "Firoz, for God's sake, will you ever send me a report free of errors? I'm fed up with this nonsense."

Firoz was taken aback at this sudden outburst from Rakesh, because he had never faced this before. Rakesh's words pierced him like poisoned arrows. The fact that Rakesh had said this to him in front of the whole team also deeply saddened and embarrassed him. He felt as if he was being called a dumb idiot. It was difficult for him to accept his mistake because Rakesh's words had attacked his self-image.

What are the alternative ways that Firoz could have reacted?

He could have become defensive. Trying to defend his self-image, he would have argued with Rakesh about how he had clearly stated that he was not good at macros during his interview, and yet he was being given tasks that required building complex macros in a very short time.

Alternatively, Firoz would have said nothing to Rakesh. But as soon as Rakesh left the scene, he would have badmouthed Rakesh and justified himself to his colleagues in an attempt to salvage his dignity. He would do this because he didn't want to own up to his mistakes for the reasons stated above. But this would mean damaging his relationship with Rakesh, which in turn would make it difficult for them to work together.

Now let us consider how Rakesh could have handled this in a more appropriate way. Firstly, since Firoz was making frequent mistakes, Rakesh should have known that if he didn't give Firoz early feedback, the situation would worsen. His own frustration would build up, and anything he would say at that point, would be misinterpreted. In an ideal case, Rakesh should have given Firoz feedback about his work at the very first or second instance in a suitable manner.

Secondly, instead of asking Firoz to come over to his cabin, he spoke to him in front of the whole team, inflicting a deeper wound on Firoz's self-image. Rakesh should have ensured to speak to Firoz in private.

Thirdly, Rakesh's manner and choice of words should have been positive and encouraging, like, "Firoz, I've noticed some errors in the reports you'd sent. I believe that's because you don't have much exposure to macros. I think it would help if you could take inputs from someone in the team or watch some YouTube videos on macros. I'm sure you'll excel at it in no time. It will help you in performing more efficiently and effectively."

Thus, Rakesh wouldn't sound bitter or angry. As he attributed Firoz's mistakes to his lack of knowledge of macros, it helped secure Firoz's self-image. Finally, Rakesh offered him a solution and also demonstrated his confidence in Firoz's capabilities.

This is an example of how people can avoid letting situations from escalating, causing severe miscommunication, and hurting others' self-image.

Communicating without hurting someone's self-image becomes especially challenging when we are trying to point out someone's mistakes or shortcomings. Criticism is not always bad or negative, but its overuse projects a predominantly negative meaning. Objecting to something, only with the purpose of proving it to be wrong, false, or mistaken, is called Negative Criticism, which is unpleasant and unwelcome. We will discuss this topic at length in a later chapter.

8

Would you be Right or Rather be Happy?

What would you rather be? A person who was right all his life but was always unhappy, or a person who was wrong all his life but was always happy?

There is an elegant simplicity to this question and a remarkable depth. It opens our eyes to the truth that this can be a conscious choice. Sometimes being right is accompanied by being happy, but in most cases the two are mutually exclusive. The need to be right becomes a hindrance to being happy.

The need to be right is important for most people, such that it becomes an obsession for them. They strive for it, even at the cost of their peace and happiness. Surely, most of us would have come across at least one such person in our life. Perhaps, we could be one ourselves!

Put yourself into such a person's shoes. How does it feel to be like them? Always struggling to prove yourself right, always justifying yourself, and being disappointed that no one understands you. Imagine the stress you will be under all the time. Acting on the constant need to be right requires considerable energy; it can be exhausting!

But when we try to prove we are right, why do conversations get so tense? This is so because unknowingly, when we say, "I am right," we are also saying, "You are wrong," and no one wants to be proven wrong. We may not say it in clear words, but the sentiment of the conversation makes the other person feel that we are trying to prove them wrong. Let us understand this with an example.

Suppose you need to dispatch a parcel urgently and you get a little late to reach the postoffice, just when the clerk is about to close it for the day.

"Can you please accept the parcel?" you ask.

"Sorry, you're late. You will need to bring this in tomorrow. Working hours are over," the clerk replies.

You glance at your watch and try to reason with him, "But closing time is still another three minutes away."

Now, the clerk is also aware of this fact. But by reasoning this way, you have proved him wrong. Although you have not actually said this in words, you have rubbed him in the wrong way. Your manner of speaking hurts his ego, causing him to shut himself down, much before shutting the counter! Once this happens, you will find it difficult to get him to cooperate. Only those with open hearts are able to help others.

During the conversation, both parties are conveying the sentiment, "I am right, and you are wrong!" Their ego stops them from accepting that they could be wrong. Each one feels that they are right and the other person is wrong. As a result, communication breaks down.

What is the solution to this? A shift of attitude.

A shift from "I am right" to "I am wrong."

Let us revisit the same conversation in the light of this shift.

"Can you please accept the parcel?" you ask.

"Sorry, you're late. You will need to bring this in tomorrow. Working hours are over."

You glance at your watch and say, "You're right, working hours are over. Actually, I had to drop my daughter at school on my way and you know how hard it is to find a decent parking space near schools! That's why I got late. I'm sorry about this, but can you please make an exception and help me out this time? This parcel is really very important and has to go out today."

The first conversation conveyed to the clerk that he was being proven wrong. In the second, he is reassured that he is right and then he is implored to help. Telling people that they are right early on in a conversation reassures them and opens their heart. Such a person will be able to empathize with your troubles and eager to help you out. It is important to learn how to open up people by the adept use of words.

Suppose you have assigned a particular task to everyone in the team, which has to be completed in a given time period. At the end of the stipulated time, you check the status with all the team members. You ask those who haven't completed the task, why they haven't. Almost everyone tries to give reasons and blame it on a person or a situation. So, in their eyes, they are right but the other person or the situation is wrong. How many do you think will own up responsibility and confess, "I was wrong. I should have completed the task in the stipulated time, but I haven't."

Observe yourself when someone tries to correct you. You will sense a feeling of insecurity. You will shut down and try to block the speaker's words. You may even feel rebellious and want to retaliate.

Once we have observed ourselves and understood what we go through, it becomes easy for us to empathize with what the other person could be going through. Hence, whenever we have to converse with someone who is being obstinate, we should first reassure him that he is right. This way, our appeals have a better chance of falling upon more receptive ears.

For some people, this manner of speaking comes naturally. They can easily admit, "I am wrong, and you are right." Such people experience that most of the time, they get help and their work gets done.

On the other end, those who keep arguing that they are right, always find that their work gets stuck. You will hear them complain about it all the time.

Both these categories of people have no idea why this happens to them, but now we know the reason.

9

Criticism is of No Help

Criticism is a common but painful experience. It triggers fear, shame, or anger, and makes one feel insecure, unworthy, and incompetent, thus harming their self-image. Criticism is harmful to relationships when it is:

- About personality or character, rather than behavior
- Filled with blame
- Not focused on improvement
- Based on only one "right way" of doing things
- Belittling

Before criticizing anyone, take a pause to assess whether you are criticizing for any of the above reasons. If it is, then refrain from it. Even if it's not the case, and if you are looking for an improvement in the other person's behavior, explore creative ways of expressing what you want to, without sounding critical.

It is not difficult to see that negative criticism doesn't really work. So why do people keep doing it, even in the face of mounting frustration? Let us understand the reasons why people criticize in the first place.

Reasons of Criticism

Reason 1 – Criticism can be a form of ego-defense. We don't always criticize because we disagree with someone's behavior or attitude. Many a time, we criticize because we somehow feel belittled by their behavior or attitude. We feel threatened in their presence. As our ego is in a vulnerable state, we defend it by criticizing or belitting them.

Two people are chatting about stock trading, buying and selling strategies. Suddenly a third person, who is very successful at trading, joins them. One of them feels threatened by him and starts criticizing the third person's trading strategies. The criticizer gets a false sense of being more knowledgeable and successful than the third person. However, due to this false and short-lived sense of superiority, he keeps criticizing others, thereby worsening his relationships. He gains the reputation of always being critical.

Reason 2 – Some people consider criticism as a necessity for growth and betterment. Their perspective is, "If I don't criticize them, how will they evolve to become better versions of themselves?!" They take it upon themselves to improve the world by way of criticism. They even go so far as to say that they too could evolve only because they were heavily criticized; that they took the criticism as a motivation for growth.

Firstly, such people need to understand that criticism can rarely succeed in achieving positive change, because criticism only focuses on what's wrong instead of how it can be made right.

Secondly, although they were able to use criticism as a springboard for their own evolution, not everyone can. Many people feel extremely dejected with constant criticism and could sink into depression at times. A few may tackle criticism head-on, but for most people, positive encouragement and words of appreciation are bound to work better than criticism. As seen in an earlier chapter, appreciating a child's painting skills and encouraging him to do better improves his painting.

In spite of all this, if one still feels criticism is necessary, words have to be carefully chosen.

For example: Instead of focusing on what's wrong by saying: Why can't you pay attention to the bills?

Give a solution by saying: Let's go over the bills together today. I'm sure you'll manage by yourself from tomorrow.

Instead of devaluing someone by saying: I guess you're just not smart enough to do this.

Encourage them by saying: I know you have a lot on your plate, but I'm pretty sure we can do this together.

Instead of implying blame by saying: It's your fault that we're in this financial mess.

Focus on the future by saying: We can get out of this situation if we both give up a few things. What do you think?

All the above examples address the same problem, but in different ways and the latter statements are sure to yield better results.

Reason 3 – The third reason for criticism is habit. Some people have been criticizing others for so long that it has now become their habit. As soon as they notice someone's flaw or mistake, they feel compelled to criticize them. They indulge in their compulsions so much that it becomes a way of life for them. Such people lead life without awareness. They learn the hard way when they are jolted awake by life's circumstances. That's when they become aware of their habit and work on controlling it.

If one has fallen prey to this habit, they should contemplate on the following before criticizing anyone:

- What is the reason behind my criticism?
- Am I criticizing to defend my ego?
- Is whatever I am about to say, the consistent truth?
- Is it absolutely necessary for me to say it?

- Can I rephrase my sentences to make them sound less hurtful, insulting, or belittling?

These questions serve like a mirror, throwing light on the real reasons behind criticism. However, if the intention is genuine, there are positive ways of saying what you want to, which can avert the ill effects of this habit of criticising.

There are many disadvantages of using criticism. At work, criticism will almost always be ill received. People who are criticized will pounce at every chance of settling the score by retaliating more hurtfully.

When parents are overtly critical of their children, the children become desensitized to their words. However, this isn't a sudden occurrence. In the initial days, parents' words do affect children, making them feel sad. But hearing the same words repeatedly, makes them develop a mechanism of dodging painful emotions by ignoring what their parents say. They grow emotionally distanced from their parents and this further frustrates the parents, sending the relationship down a spiral.

In their early years, children's self-image is still in a developing stage. It is fragile and vulnerable to the experiences that the child has to endure. At such a stage, if the child is subjected to constant criticism, it can prove damaging to their self-image and confidence.

People who are over-criticized as children, grow up to have a very weak self-image and are likely to become severe critics themselves. Not many children retaliate to their parents when they are criticized. They tend to stay quiet on the outside, but keep seething within, and this pressure gradually impacts their self-image.

Some parents tend to compare their children with their siblings or other children, who are better at academics or sports. They say things like, "Why can't you be like him? He's so talented at Maths and you're afraid of even the simplest sums!", "I don't think you're going to get anywhere with Cricket. You might as well give it up and try something else!"

Parents' words have a profound impact on the child's mind because they unquestioningly trust their parents. Children grow up thinking that they are less talented and physically weaker than others. Imagine the disastrous effect of criticism on such children. Many of them are required to undergo extensive therapies in their adulthood to break free of their limiting beliefs. Hence, it is imperative for parents to be very careful when communicating with their children.

Having discussed negative criticism and its effects, you may wonder whether there is any alternative to it. Since criticism is sure to be received badly, should we not point out others' mistakes at all? Should we ignore them and just keep moving on?

No! Instead of criticizing, we can criti*guide*! Instead of pointing out the wrong, we can point in the right direction by using the right words. Critiguiding is the right way of giving feedback. It is an essential skill if we want to help our near and dear ones improve.

Let us take a deeper look at critiguiding in the next chapter.

10

Critiguiding – Part 1

Simply put, critiguiding is positive criticism with empathy. It is when one points out others' mistakes in an empathetic manner, after understanding the following:

- It is the mistake or flaw that is bad, not the person. Hence, separate the mistake or the flaw from the person to address it.
- Any hurtful words I say, may hurt his self-image and damage our relationship. So, I need to be very careful about what I say and how I say it.
- I have no anger, resentment, or jealousy for him and whatever I am about to say is purely out of genuine care and compassion.
- I won't focus on what is wrong but will convey an action plan to fix the problem and will encourage him to put the plan in action.

You will know when you have successfully critiguided someone. You will feel the positive energy building around the conversation and the person will automatically focus on the solution instead of the problem.

There are six different ways in which one can critiguide. We will discuss three of them in this chapter.

1. Say it without saying it

Navin, a sixth grader, had received his progress card at school and he was required to get his parents' signature on it. He had done well in all the other subjects, but Maths had been a particularly bad test, and the grades reflected it. He went home, worrying about how his mother would react to his Maths grades. His mother was speaking to someone on the phone. He went and held the progress card in front of her, fully expecting to be scolded. His mother excused herself on the phone, hung up and took the card from Navin.

"You've done well in Social Studies. That's nice! Your English is getting better. I like that! Science has always been your strength. Fantastic! Physical Education is better than it was last semester. Good!"

Saying this, she signed the progress card and handed it back to Navin. Navin was surprised she had mentioned every subject except Maths. Do you think Navin might not have realized this? Of course, he did. Children are very perceptive. If communicated in the right way, they are capable of understanding and working on any problem.

By not saying a word about his Maths score, Navin's mother had silently told him that she was not happy about Maths and that he had to work hard on it. And that is exactly what Navin understood too. This method communicates that you have confidence in the other person's perceptiveness. His mother demonstrated this fact and believed in her son's capability to take corrective steps without the need to scold or yell at him. Showing such confidence and trust in the child strengthens their self-image.

Many parents consider it necessary to scold their children to fix their mistakes, some even justify punishing them. But being subjected to such treatment repeatedly, desensitizes children to it. On the contrary, parents who constantly communicate positively and compassionately with their children and have open and constructive discussions with them, can use even their silence to make a remarkable impression on their child. Their silence has a positive impact because their words have a positive impact as well. The same isn't applicable to a parent who always scolds the child. When a scolding parent keeps quiet, it is almost a relief to the child!

Here is another example of how being silent about something can be a better form of communication than verbalizing it. A woman cooked her husband's favorite dish for dinner. But she mistakenly added too much salt to it. When they sat for dinner, she insisted that he eat first, eager about his reaction to the dish. As soon as he tasted the first morsel, he blurted out, "Oh God! Too much salt... this is not tasting good!" Now by pointing out her mistake, he was proving her wrong. As a result, her self-image and sentiments were hurt.

Was there a way to communicate this without actually verbalizing it? Yes, there was! The husband could have chosen not to say anything about it or simply appreciating her thought of making his favorite dish. His wife too was going to eat it eventually and then she would come to know about the excess salt herself. As the mistake was not verbalized, there would be a two-pronged effect. One, the wife would appreciate her husband for not pointing it out as a mistake and belittling her efforts. And two, she would be encouraged to do better the next time.

Hence, before you criticize someone, it helps to consider whether silence is an option. Are there chances that the other person will come to realize their mistake in spite of your silence? If yes, then always choose silence over words. After all, we've already discussed how speech is silver, while silence is golden!

2. Sandwich Technique

Sandwiching your criticism between two positive or encouraging statements is a very good way to critiguide someone without making them feel bad. Start by appreciating, then state the mistake, offer a solution, and then close the conversation with another positive remark or by verbalizing your confidence in the listener's ability to apply the solution.

For example, consider a father who wants to tell his little daughter that she needs to be consistent with her studies. He can pick a moment when she is already studying and tell her, "Wow! Your handwriting is beautiful! And I've noticed that you've been sincerely studying for so long. That's great. You are intelligent. All you have to do is make studying a regular habit and you'll be soaring!"

Using the Sandwich technique also demonstrates that we are not out to solely criticize people. With a little study and practice, we can make it a habit to use this technique anywhere.

At work, instead of bluntly pointing a mistake to a colleague or subordinate, we can use this technique to make a positive impact. "I love the creativity you put into your tasks. The presentation you sent me yesterday was excellent! The way you've structured the points and visually presented them in the slides is impressive! If you could only conquer deadlines, I'm sure your work will prove to be even more effective. Your presentation slides will enable me to impress our clients and bag the order. Keep up the good work!"

Far from making the listener feel bad, such communication encourages them to work upon themselves and do better each time. This is a great way to demonstrate your trust in people.

3. Express opinions, not verdicts

There are a very few things under the sun that can be called universal truths. Nearly everything else is open to interpretation. Everyone can have a different opinion. In fact, the diversity of opinions is necessarily what keeps the world going! Many a time, when we say something to someone, we assume it to be the universal truth, whereas it need not always be true. If the listener has a different take on that subject, we are already proving him wrong! But when we express it as our opinion, we respect the listener's right to have his own view, whether or not to accept that view is a different matter. You can even clearly state your intention by saying, "This is what I feel, you may have a different view."

By expressing our thoughts as an opinion and not a final verdict, we keep the listener's heart and mind open, so that they may genuinely consider our words and think about them. By stating a verdict, our arrogant words most definitely render the listener's ears deaf and his mind closed!

11
Critiguiding – Part 2

In the previous chapter, we have considered three ways of critiguiding. Now, we will look at the other three subtler ways of critiguiding people, so as to help them overcome their flaws and bring out their best.

1. Indirect communication

Indirect communication may prove helpful when one is trying to attempt a gentle "letdown." Indirect communication is based on the trust that the listener will figure out the import of the message, without it being explicitly mentioned.

Here is an example. Arun was returning from a meeting with a multinational company. He had come to know that his company's project proposal had been rejected because the multinational company was unwilling to work with a small establishment. Although his company was much smaller than the multinational company, it was specialized in a particular domain, unlike the multinational company that had its fingers in many pies. Arun was worried about how he would communicate the reason of rejection to Jay. Saying it on Jay's face might land him in trouble.

When he reached office, Jay called him to his cabin and asked him about the rejection.

"Looks like they want to work with a jack-of-all, not a master-of-one!" Arun replied.

Jay excused him without replying at that time, but later when he realized how Arun had managed an awkward conversation, he called him back and heartily appreciated him. Arun had conveyed the perception that they had given a good proposal, but it wasn't their mistake if the multinational company didn't want to work with a small-but-specialised establishment like them. In this way, he had successfully used indirect communication to gently convey something negative.

An indirect communication has to be balanced. While one has to avoid the direct approach, one also cannot be excessively vague and risk a gross misunderstanding.

If a subordinate is getting late to work every day, instead of confronting him with, "Why do you come late every day?" or "When will you learn to be on time?" you can say, "Let's have a meeting at 9 a.m. tomorrow. I will let you run the meeting so that you may take over that responsibility from now on. Does that sound good to you?"

By setting the meeting time at 9 a.m. and handing him the charge for the meeting, you are indirectly communicating that he needs to be on time. He too is aware of the fact that coming late to work every day is wrong. However, instead of accusing him directly, you can use this method to ensure that he sets course for correction and comes on time from the next day. This way, he too appreciates the fact that he was not reprimanded.

2. Appreciate in public, and critiguide in private

Appreciation should be public and criticism private. But most people tend to do the opposite. They appreciate others when they are alone and criticize them in front of everyone.

Everyone likes to be positively perceived by others. We treat others according to the perception we carry about them. Hence, when we criticize someone in public, it hurts not only their self-image but also their projected image. Consequently, they grow bitter and stop listening to us, even if we say something positive. However, if we speak to them when they are alone, they may not mind that so much.

Suppose your subordinate makes a careless mistake. Everyone in the office perceives him as an efficient team member and respects his seniority. He is also naturally eager to preserve this image. You meet him in the office lobby, but lead him to your desk and speak to him in private about correcting his mistake. He appreciates that you chose not to malign his image by rebuffing him in front of other colleagues. And given this opportunity, he also makes a sincere effort to not repeat his mistake again.

When doctors need to communicate to a patient about a serious illness, they do so in private, not in front of everyone. It is their way of extending their help to the patient to preserve his external image. In this way, speaking to people when they are alone is the only appropriate way to guide them.

While speaking to people when they are alone, we should also tell them that they are not the only one to make such a mistake or have such a flaw. This can prove to be a very important help.

For example, if your child is trying to learn cricket and is not able to throw the ball properly, you can tell him, "You know, when I was small, I too used to find it difficult to throw the ball in the right direction. But I practiced and got better at it. I'm sure you can do the same!" Now, regardless of whether this is true or not, it surely gives the child a feeling of relief, thinking that he is not the only one to have that problem, that it is normal to have such problems or make such mistakes. This feeling boosts his courage and confidence to conquer the problem.

Someone who needs to learn to type faster can be told, "Your typing is absolutely error-free; proofreading is not at all necessary. All you have to do is learn techniques to speed up your typing, so that you can complete the work in lesser time." Further, you can say, "I was also pretty bad at typing. But I learnt some techniques to increase my typing speed and could manage to improve it. I'm sure you can also do the same."

3. Speak the language that people understand

Does that mean I should only speak to people in their mother tongue? No! The meaning of language in this context is the manner of speaking. So, speak to people in a manner that they'll like or understand. Here's a little joke that illustrates this point.

A man had fallen into a deep pit and was crying out desperately for help. People who were passing by, wondered where the cries were coming from and found that they were coming from the pit. Finding the man deep inside, many of them extended their hands to him saying, "Give me your hand... Give me your hand." But to everyone's surprise, despite his cries for help, it didn't seem like he wanted to be rescued at all. People tried to look around to find a rope or a stick, but nothing could be found and here this man was just not cooperating. He was crying for help, but he wouldn't give his hand.

Just then, another person who was passing by, came to the pit and saw what was happening. Holding out his hand like others, he yelled out, "Here... take my hand." To everyone's amazement, the man in the pit immediately grabbed onto his hands and was pulled out.

Later, when people asked him how he was able to get the man to hold out his hands, he said, "It's funny you know... That man was my neighbor a few years ago and he is one hell of a miser. Didn't you notice that I said, 'Take my hand' and not 'Give me your hand' like you all were saying? He doesn't recognize the language of 'giving', he only knows the language of 'taking'! That's why he 'took' my hand, but refused to 'give' his hand to you'll!"

Jokes apart, this story illustrates that while helping people, you have to speak *their* language to assure them that you genuinely want to help them. For this, you have to place yourself in their shoes and think, "What words would I like to hear if I were them? How would I like to be spoken to, so as to feel the need to act upon the words?"

We have seen the six ways of critiguiding that help in preventing standoffs in relationships and motivate people to improve themselves. We need to observe ourselves in situations when we criticize others and introspect on how we can creatively critiguide them.

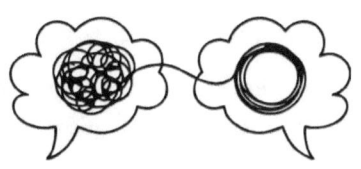

PART 3
COMMUNICATION IN THE FAMILY

Sending Rays of Healing Light

We all know that simply sitting and worrying for others doesn't achieve anything. Yet, family members are often found incessantly worrying about each other, especially the elders about the young ones.

It is natural for us to worry about the ones we care about. But instead of worrying, what can we do that will actually be of some help? We can send them rays of healing light! Sending healing rays is the best alternative to worrying about someone.

Let us understand what sending healing rays means and how it benefits. Whenever you find yourself worrying about someone, close your eyes and bring the person you were worrying about to the forefront of your attention. Visualize rays of white healing light projecting on them. Mentally say these words repeatedly: "May God bless you with love, joy, peace, and good health."

If you have just had an argument with some family member or friend, you can add, "Please forgive me for whatever I had said or done to hurt you. I too forgive you for any hurt you have caused me. From now on, we shall get along in harmony."

Sending them the healing rays and saying these words will have a magical effect. White rays of light are symbolic of health, joy, compassion, abundance, love, and peace. By imagining white rays falling on them, we wish for all these positive attributes to rain down upon them. The healing rays have a definite effect on them.

This works regardless of what the other person has said or done to you or what he is thinking about you at that moment. What is important is that by sending healing light, you initiate a positive change in the state of your relationship.

12

Forming a Platform for Communication

Usually, family members always care about each other. They want to grow together, laugh together, live happily together. No one wants to cause sorrow or pain to any other member. They are even willing to take on each other's troubles or challenges. And yet, even in such families, arguments do happen. Isn't that a surprising contrast?!

A little research and contemplation will clarify the cause and the solution. One of the most important causes of familial tensions is the lack of communication. Naturally, the solution is better communication. If everyone in the family were to exercise good communication and listening skills, such a family will achieve a greatly enhanced co-existence with love and happiness.

If we first understand why frictions and arguments occur in families, it can help us improve our communication in the family. The reason is simple: they are not listening to each other.

Imagine you're sitting in the drawing room watching TV and your brother is in his bedroom studying. Your brother calls out to you, asking you to get some water. On his first call, you do not hear him because the TV is turned on loud. He calls out again and the second time you do hear him, but you ignore him because the program you're watching is at a pivotal and interesting juncture and you do not want to miss it. So, you continue watching the TV. Your brother calls out a third time—this time a little louder and angrier. You get irritated, get up, and stomp to his bedroom and… anyone can guess the kind of conversation that will follow.

Now let us change the setting of this incident a little bit. Imagine you're in a hospital. Your brother is admitted and is lying on the bed. You're outside the room, watching some video on your phone. This time, will you wait till he calls out for water the third time? Wouldn't you rush in the very first time he calls out? What causes such a big shift in your response? This is so because you can see the physical state that your brother is in. You can see that he is lying on a bed, probably in pain and in great need of water. You care about him.

Someone's physical state of being is very clearly visible. Hence it becomes easy for us to give an appropriate response. Someone is on a hospital bed, someone is enjoying music, eating food, arguing on the phone, listening to a joke, dressing a wound—these are all physical states of being that are very clear, and one will intuitively know how to respond in each of them.

But how about the mental state of being? That is not always very clear. A housewife can be seen cooking lunch, but mentally she could be worried about her father's health. Another person can be seen eating popcorn at a movie, but mentally he could possibly be worried about the office meeting that's scheduled the next day.

Since we are unable to see someone's mental state of being as clearly as we see their physical state of being, we give the wrong response to the person. And so, tensions and frictions arise. This is the gravest and most common problem in familial communication. Each one is looking at a different picture.

When an argument breaks, all the family members involved fail to see that each one of them is viewing the subject from a different perspective. It is just a problem of non-alignment of perspectives. The solution is simply to align them! But how can that be achieved? By creating a platform for communication. Let us see how.

When Samir was a schooler, his teacher had called him an "idiot" in front of the whole class. Everyone had laughed and Samir had shrunk deep into his desk, feeling insulted. The incident had made such a deep impression on his mind, that much later, even as an adult, he could not hear the word "idiot" without arousing the same feelings of hurt and humiliation.

He married Anita. Anita was in the habit of saying the word "idiot" casually. She was not aware of Samir's aversion to the word. A couple of times, she playfully called him an idiot, to which Samir got very upset. To Anita's surprise, he reacted angrily, thus leading to arguments. The arguments that began there, started spreading to other parts of their lives, creating a rift between them.

Both, Anita and Samir, had a different perspective about the word and both were seeing their own perspectives only. Had Samir known the importance of creating a platform for communication in the family, he would have spent time with Anita to explain how he had come to hate that word so much and the effect it had on him. Their perspectives could have fallen into alignment. Anita, being a caring wife, would have surely understood his plight and would have been careful not to use that word around Samir, especially in reference to him. This would have saved them from countless arguments and the rift between them. Also, when a spouse opens up about his fears and vulnerabilities to his partner, the partner feels valued and wanted.

Many families experience a lot of friction and tension due to lack of a communication platform. If all the family members were to come together to form such a platform, imagine the multitudes of problems that can be solved!

What is the best time to form a communication platform?

We have all heard the proverb "One shouldn't dig a well when one is thirsty." It shows the lack of awareness and preparedness about the problem at hand. One of Albert Einstein's famous quotes says, "One cannot solve a problem from the same mindset that created it." In the same way, one cannot form a communication platform when some incident has just occurred, and everyone is disturbed. The best time to get to work on this is when everyone is in the best of their spirits. This is like a preparation for the times when incidents occur.

The following questions should be discussed beforehand on a family platform and every family member, however young or old, must get a say in this discussion.

- What does each person like and dislike hearing? It is especially important to discuss things and words that each person doesn't like because it is more important to first take care of things that annoy others and later focus on things that they like.
- How each person would prefer to be dealt with when he or she is angry, sad, or frustrated.
- How each member would like or more importantly dislike being treated when the family is hosting guests or is out being a guest.

All frequently occurring arguments, like those regarding the TV, spending money, behavior of each family member, indiscriminate use of smartphones etc., should be discussed on this platform well before they actually occur. This gives each family member a chance to present their side. A solution for each should also be discussed and actioned so that arguments are avoided. A family that can achieve this, can endure the toughest of challenges without a communication breakdown.

A discussion platform is also necessary to give family members a chance to modify the way they talk to or behave with one another. For example, a father may think it necessary to act strictly with his teenage son, who he thinks turns a deaf ear to his words. And the son turns a deaf ear to his father because he doesn't like the way he is spoken to. This is a catch-22 situation that can only be resolved by bringing both the father and son to a common platform and getting them to talk openly to each other. Only then can the father tell the son that he acts strictly only to make his son listen to him for things that he considers important for his son. The son can openly share that he is being rebellious only because he doesn't like to be treated as a little child. The father will then realize that the simple way to bring about a positive change in his son's behavior would be to treat him like an adult.

When such open and honest discussions happen on a common platform in families, they can define the methods of communication to be used when they are in a crisis and thus emerge successful together.

Thus, having understood the importance of forming a communication platform, let us now look at a few ideas of a communication platform.

1. Use a code language

A code language—the meaning of which is only known to the family members—is an excellent way to form a common platform of communication. This method is especially useful when non-family guests or friends are present, and the family wants to communicate with each other without their knowledge and without making it obvious to them. For example, a husband may want to communicate something exclusively to his wife while his friends are visiting.

A famous film personality from India shared a similar example in an interview. He shared that when he was young, he loved it when they had guests visiting, because it meant that delicious food would be served, that he would get to enjoy too. While he was eager to eat the food, his mother had to be careful not to let the food fall short for the guests. But to make sure this didn't happen, she couldn't just ask her children to stop eating in front of the guests. So, she developed a unique code language. Whenever she thought that the food stock may fall short, she would tell her children, "FHB... FHB..." Now the visiting guests or friends would not know the meaning of this, but the children would know that she meant to say, "Family hold back." This would give them the signal that there is less food. And when there was enough food she would say, "FGA... FGA..."

which meant "Family go ahead" or "Family, eat as much as you want."

Here are some examples of codes that will give you an idea of how you can develop your own system for coded communication.

Code	Meaning
Moon	Out of budget / Too expensive.
CO	Let's check out other shops for this item.
NN	Not now.
Magic	If you behave well now, you'll get a gift later.
East West	Please don't ask questions, just help or do your task.
Lifeline	Please leave me alone to decide what to do.
TC	Take charge, handle the situation.

Examples of coded communication for embarrassing situations:

Code	Meaning
Update your status	There's a stain on your clothes / Zip is open.
Lock your mobile	Your shirt / trouser / dress is torn.
Gas prices have gone up	You've eaten too much. Enough already!
Let's play music!	Don't make that smacking noise while eating.
Change your ringtone	Don't reveal the incidents of my past.

In this way, every family can come up with their own unique codes that form a platform for encoded communication.

2. Use gestures or postures

Sometimes it may not be possible to use words or sounds as code language. In such cases, gestures or postures can be used to convey messages. For example, you can touch your ears to communicate to someone to stay silent and listen. You can rub your eyes to communicate that it is time to leave. You can cross your legs or keep them straight to mean different things.

Here are some examples of gestures that can be used:

Code	Meaning
Tossing a coin	Relax, don't worry and think positively.
Touching one's ear	Listen carefully to what's being said.
Rub one's eyes	Let's leave now.
Tapping foot	Please talk less.
Make a fist	Control your emotions.

3. Fridge magnets

Sometimes a member of the family is in a very talkative mood and wants to chat with another family member about something. But the other member may not be in a mood for conversation. He or she may be either worried about something or in a contemplative mood, wanting to be left alone. In such cases, if the former tries to speak with the latter without knowing the latter's mood, it may lead to frustration and miscommunication.

Not all family members are able to openly communicate their moods verbally. Hence, families with whom such incidents occur frequently, need some kind of a non-verbal system which will help in communicating each family member's mood. This can be done with the help of fridge magnets.

Put up little chits with the names of all family members on the fridge and place a fridge magnet against each name. The family can discuss and decide what colors would indicate which mood. For example, a red fridge magnet would indicate anger, yellow will indicate normal mood, and green will mean a happy mood. There can be more colors for other moods as well. This method is especially important when everybody is expected to be at home, like in the evening. So, once someone comes home, they can first go to the fridge to check how everyone's mood is and then communicate accordingly. This will prevent frictions due to mood differences among family members. Additionally, if someone is angry, another family member can try to talk to them about it (in a predetermined way in which the family member likes to be spoken to when they're angry) to make them feel better.

4. Adopt a meeting culture in the family

Meeting culture is an effective way of bringing all family members together. A regularly held family meeting can be used as a platform to openly discuss and solve anything—from trivial matters to major crises—just like companies hold meetings to solve work related problems.

A healthy discussion during meetings can help address complaints that family members have for each other. Most people are worried that such meetings may lead to heated arguments. But if each member exercises restraint, a common platform can be formed, wherein every member will get a fair opportunity to speak out what they feel without any fear or obligation.

Free speech is the key aspect of a communication platform. Members should be able to freely express their feelings instead of giving partial revelations for the fear of inviting an argument. Such meetings will also foster qualities of attentive listening, patience, and forbearance in all the members of the family since everyone has to listen to everyone else.

Remember that the goal of such meetings is not to point out each other's mistakes and criticize, but to improve relations between family members. Generally, people look at improving others without thinking about their own improvement. But in family meetings, the focus will be on listening to and understanding others rather than improving them. Then the meetings can turn out to be successful.

5. Communicating with children

Parents often tell their children what they should and shouldn't be doing, but how much do the children actually understand and implement it? Probably very little; hence the large number of disgruntled parents. New age children and teens are not satisfied with being told what to do or what not to do. They also want to know the reason behind it. To every suggestion, command, or request from their parents, they will question "Why?" And until they get a satisfactory answer, they find it difficult to oblige.

Whenever you ask your child to do or not do something, add your feelings to the conversation to complete the communication. For example, if your six-year-old is doing somersaults on the bed and you're afraid he may topple and hurt himself, tell him, 'Please don't do that on the bed. If you lose your balance, you might fall and hurt yourself. Then I will be very sad!" This totally conveys your feelings to your child, and he is more likely to stop doing what he is doing.

Here is another example. A mother of two teenage daughters noticed that they were constantly busy using their smartphones or tablets. She kept telling them repeatedly about the ill effects of overuse of phones and tabs, but they continued unhindered.

One day, she sat her daughters down and said, "Girls, I have been trying to tell you not to use your phones for such long hours. Staring at the little screen and listening to such loud music inside your ears for long hours can affect you and eventually lead to health issues. And if anything were to happen to you, I will be devastated!"

After this conversation, she noticed that both her daughters reduced the use of their phones and tabs. In this way, instead of trying to control their children, if parents give them the right understanding through right communication, they will have a much better future. The best thing a parent can do for a child is to listen to them, fully and attentively. Give them the freedom to pour out everything that's on their mind. Let them speak about themselves, about you, about anything, but let them freely express!

13
Glass Breaking

When two people stop communicating with each other, they start slowly growing apart. With the passage of time, the rift deepens to such an extent that there comes a point when they find it extremely difficult to start communicating with each other.

Many a time, this hesitation keeps people from trying further, thus leading to something like a glass wall between them. This glass wall cannot be seen, but can be felt as a hesitation and awkwardness when either of them try to reach out to the other. Such relationships begin to get bitter with time. The glass wall gets thicker and increasingly difficult to break. Note that the word used here is "difficult," not "impossible"! Hence, it is wise to break a glass wall before it gets too thick.

Imagine a family where the father and son have not communicated since a long time because of some past incident. They live in different cities, so they are further estranged. Both have been trying to make an attempt to speak to each other, but hesitation holds them back. Both of them have dialed the number and disconnected immediately, giving up.

Then one day, the son learns about glass breaking in a self-improvement course and decides to implement it. Later that day, after dinner, he picks up the phone determinedly and makes the call. Making up his mind to go through with the conversation, he waits for his father to answer. When his father does, he says, "Dad, I know we haven't spoken since a long time, but I've been wanting to say this to you since a few days. Whatever happens between us, I want you to know that I will always love and respect you for who you are. I can never repay you for all that you've done for me, for fulfilling all my needs and wants ever since I was little. But I want to thank you and tell you that you're the best father I have ever known!"

A long silence follows, which is then broken by the father's choked words, "I love you too son!" The father couldn't say much more, but one can imagine how the glass wall between them was shattered and communication was unblocked again! It's not that family members stop loving and caring for each other. The love is still there; they still care for each other, it's just that these emotions have stayed unexpressed for too long.

It is more common for people to express their anger, frustration, disappointment or resentment more frequently than their love or gratitude. It is not always wrong to express our negative emotions to our family members, but overdoing the one without doing the other, disturbs the balance in relationships. In fact, the more one expresses negative emotions, the more one should consciously express the positive ones as well. Expectation is a basic human tendency and non-fulfilment of expectations leads to disappointments and rifts. So, in the weighing balance of relationships, the side of disappointment always weighs heavier.

Some people may argue that they carry certain expectations for some others purely out of compassion for their betterment. Like a father's expectation from his son or daughter to behave in a particular way or do certain things. In the end, it is true that fulfilling their father's expectations is going to be beneficial for the children themselves. But the problem here is that very often, when expectations are not fulfilled, people express their disappointment, but do not express their love and compassion that were the underlying reasons for those expectations. The end result is that only disappointment is expressed.

Some people feel uncomfortable verbalizing their love and compassion to others. The father may think, "Why do I need to explicitly say it? Of course, I love my children and want them to be the best they can be! But saying it in words sounds cheap to me."

This is what happens with most relations. Love is mostly expressed only about once or twice a year, on a birthday or during a festival. A greeting card or a gift that says, "I love you and care for you!" and that's about it.

But the love between relationships has to be expressed every day. One cannot water a plant only once a year and expect it to bloom. It has to be nurtured every day. Likewise, relationships have to be nurtured with love and gratitude as frequently as possible for them to blossom and become mutually nourishing. By expressing their love for each other more frequently, family members can feel and make others feel loved all the time. This ensures that channels of communication are always open, and the glass wall is never formed in the first place.

Let us now discuss the different ways in which one can go about glass-breaking with one's family members. The word "GLASS" itself is an acronym that will help us remember these ways.

G for Gratitude – The word "gratitude" comes from the Latin word *gratia*, which means grace, graciousness, or gratefulness. Gratitude is a thankful appreciation for what one receives, whether tangible or intangible. With gratitude, people acknowledge the goodness in their lives. We express our gratitude by saying "thanks" to someone who has helped us, given us a gift, or added value to our life in one of million different ways.

However, gratitude is not just an act, it is a selfless act, a positive emotion that serves a bigger purpose. It is a deeper appreciation for someone (or something) that further produces long lasting positivity. It gives both the speaker and the listener a deep sense of joy and satisfaction.

Expressing gratitude can do wonders for glass breaking. Appreciating family members, thanking them for being in our life, for adding value to our life, can foster a sincere, heartfelt interaction. It strengthens our relationship, and gives meaning to the lives of both—the giver of gratitude and the recipient.

L for Listening – Listening, as already discussed, is a very important part of communication and can be considered one of the pillars of the communication platform that families should have. One of the great ways to breaking the glass is to just listen to someone attentively. One of the most valuable gifts we can give someone is our time and attention.

Whoever you are trying to break the glass with, ask them engaging questions to make them talk about things they're interested in and then patiently and attentively listen to them. If someone is finding it too difficult or awkward to talk, this is an excellent method. You don't have to do any talking, just the opposite! Allow them to express whatever they have felt in the past, without reacting. Listening to someone gives them a healing experience, making them feel a deep sense of completion and satisfaction.

A for Appreciation – Everyone likes to be appreciated. Appreciating someone is a surefire way of improving relationships. Try and experiment with it: imagine someone is approaching you with the purpose of starting an argument about something, and you greet him with an appreciation, "Oh, what a beautiful tie! Is that new?", "You look different today, have you been going to the gym?" Notice how the intensity of his negative emotion fades away after you appreciate him. With the right amount of sincere appreciation, any resentment can even go away completely!

S for Sorry – There is a famous quote that says, "Saying sorry doesn't always mean that you're wrong. It means you value your relationship more than your ego." This quote illustrates a very important quality that is worth possessing – humility.

Our ego should never be a hindrance to our ability to say "I'm sorry!" Apologizing opens the doors to communication, which allows you to reconnect with the person who was hurt. It also allows you to express regret that they have been hurt, which lets them know you really care about their feelings. This can help them feel safer with you again.

A husband took his wife's help during their financial struggles for granted for the first three years of their marriage, never thanking her for all the efforts and adjustments she made to make ends meet. He would occasionally even criticize her for not doing enough. Finally, in the fourth year of their marriage, when things had started looking up, he finally realized his mistake. Better late than never, he expressed his heartfelt apology and gratitude to his wife for everything she had done for them. Imagine what the two must have felt, looking in each other's eyes!

When you seek forgiveness from someone, you bring peace not only to them, but also to yourself. Hence, never shy away from saying "I'm sorry."

S for Saying "I love you!" – It is surprising how many problems and tensions in a family can be solved by saying a genuine, "I love you!" or by expressing your love in any other simple way. When you love someone, even if you believe that it's unnecessary to say it, the truth remains that it is important to frequently verbalize it. Family members will never know how much you love them, unless you tell them.

Here are some sentences one can say to one's family regularly to make them feel cherished:

- I am inspired every time I think about my family! You guys are an inspiration to me!
- Thanks to you all, I can feel my worries diminishing and my happiness soaring!
- Coming home to you all gives such a peaceful and settling feeling!
- My family is my treasure, my greatest blessing!
- You are the best husband/wife/child/children ever!
- You are special to me and will always be!
- I feel safe sharing my secrets with you (all).
- I love you and respect you the way you are!

14

Feeling Secure in Communication

In this chapter, we shall discuss how the feeling of insecurity becomes a hurdle in communication, and why making your listener feel safe is so important.

If the listener feels insecure at the beginning of a conversation, it is likely that the conversation will soon get derailed. The listener could become suspicious that the speaker might accuse him, attack him, or capitalize on his vulnerability any moment. He goes into a defensive stance at the first instance and fiercely opposes the speaker, thus getting into a non-listening mode and the conversation gets derailed.

In such situations, whenever we feel that the listener's feeling of security is absent or diminishing, we need to first take steps to restore it, so that communication doesn't break down. Often, even before we start the conversation, we realize that the topic at hand is sensitive. So, it is likely that the listener may feel insecure and become defensive. In such a scenario, we should first make him feel secure and only then dive into the discussion.

When they decided to get married, Nisha made it clear to Karan that she would never leave her hometown. That's where her parents, her friends, and her job were, and she was not comfortable going away from all that. They had agreed upon it and got married, but soon after the marriage, they hit a bad financial patch. Karan lost his job and wasn't getting another one, however hard he tried.

In desperation, Karan started applying for job positions to companies in other cities and states. Finally, he got a lucrative job offer from a company in the neighboring state. They were offering more money than his previous job and a better designation as well. But Karan was far from being relieved, for now he had to face the more difficult task of convincing Nisha to leave the town. He knew how much the town meant to her, being born and brought up there. But he also knew how important this job was to bring back their financial stability. From his perspective, this was an imperative step for the betterment of his family.

Finally, he gathered the courage and broached the topic with her. Nisha had an inkling of what Karan was doing and was already apprehensive about this discussion.

"Nisha, we need to talk about relocating," Karan said.

As soon as he started the topic, insecurity got the better of Nisha and she retaliated, "Karan, I had clearly told you at the very outset that I'm never going to leave town. You're forgetting what we'd agreed before we decided to get married." Karan tried to explain to her that he did remember the promise, but this was necessary to keep them financially solvent, but Nisha was not listening to him at all. Getting increasingly frustrated at her stubbornness, Karan declared that they were leaving the following weekend, whether she liked it or not. Nisha reacted by storming out of the room.

Let us analyze what the two would have undergone internally. Karan knew that Nisha would not like the idea of relocating and that she would resist it. Despite knowing this, he did nothing to address her insecurity upon broaching such a sensitive topic. When he started justifying his decision to move, she started feeling increasingly insecure, perceiving his actions as a betrayal. She started believing that Karan had forgotten his promise, whereas he firmly believed that taking this decision was important for both of them. She started feeling that Karan didn't care about her, while he was wondering why she was being so stubborn and refusing to understand the situation.

Thus, any conversation—especially a sensitive one—is bound to deteriorate if the listener has not been made to feel secure. Let us look at three things one can do, to make the other person feel safe.

1. **Use safe-starters:** Very often, even before we begin a conversation, we can sense that the other person is going to feel uncomfortable about the topic. Despite knowing this, if we begin our conversation by getting straight to the point, the listener will get defensive and the conversation will not progress. Thus, it is important to make the listener feel relaxed and assured of your good intentions beforehand.

   Gauge the level of the listener's discomfort and begin by using a safe-starter that is specifically aimed at diffusing their feeling of insecurity. What are safe-starters? They are phrases or sentences you can say to make your listener feel safe and assured. Here are some examples of safe-starters:

   - Please do not misunderstand my questions. I have absolutely no doubt in my mind about your capabilities whatsoever.

   - Please take what I am about to say as a suggestion, not as criticism. I am a great admirer of your work.

   - I promise you that whatever I am about to tell you, has not made the slightest impact on how I think of you. Our relationship will be exactly how it has been before.

   - Please understand that I'm not saying you've done anything wrong. I'm sure you've followed the set system. But we need to consider exactly what steps you followed to understand what has gone wrong.

   - Please know that I do not intend to accuse you of anything. I am just communicating my thoughts to you.

   - I trust you and I know you would never want to cause anyone any harm, but if there has been a mistake for some justified reason, please tell me frankly so that we may work on fixing it together.

Using such sentences to start your conversation will ensure that the listener feels comfortable, relaxed, and safe, and the conversation has a better chance of succeeding.

2. **Convey your flexibility clearly:** If we begin a sensitive conversation in an aggressive tone, it demonstrates our rigidity and obstinacy. This makes the listener go on the defensive because he or she feels we are trying to thrust our thoughts or decisions on them. Rigidity is seldom welcome in any conversation. Thus, to make sure we are able to communicate successfully, always convey that you are flexible about your thoughts and decisions, and would like to take into consideration your listener's views on the matter too.

In the case of Karan and Nisha, Karan started the conversation by getting straight to the point. The way he put across his point was decisive and inflexible. So, Nisha responded likewise. Had he first taken some time to make her feel safe and comfortable and then assured her that this was a decision they had to take together, she may have felt much less defensive and betrayed. Here's what he could have said:

"Nisha, I know how much you love this city and how much you hate the idea of having to relocate. I know you saw this coming, and I want to assure you that I'm suggesting this as the very last resort after having tried everything else I can. I fully understand your resistance to this idea. I probably would have felt the same, had I been in your place. But please be assured that we're not going to decide anything until we both agree upon it."

This conversation starter would find her in a much more open and empathetic frame of mind. Firstly, he is reminding her beforehand that he remembers his promise to never relocate. Secondly, he assures her that the decision isn't final and that her views are as important to him as his own.

Given a chance to decide together, Nisha may even reconsider her decision of never relocating, because she now feels safe with Karan. Thus, conveying your flexibility and openness further reassures your listener, giving you a better chance of getting your point across.

3. **Create a Common Objective:** In any conversation, a listener feels insecure when they realize (or know beforehand) that your goal is the opposite of theirs. Your assertiveness shows them a picture of your goal getting fulfilled and theirs remaining unfulfilled. This fear of non-fulfillment drives them to become aggressively defensive.

   Hence, it is very important to acknowledge each other's goals to have a successful conversation. When we acknowledge the listener's objectives and convey that we care about it and also want it to be fulfilled, they feel reassured and settle down to hear us out. In such an opposite-goals situation, it helps to negotiate and arrive at a common objective so that both the parties communicate and work towards it.

   If there is a way in which the goals of both the speaker and the listener can be fulfilled, that should be discussed. Alternatively, if it is possible for both the parties to compromise a little and arrive at a common goal, that should be sought after. Thus, when both the parties look at a common goal, the feeling of security is reinstated and none of them feel victimized.

   Karan and Nisha could have negotiated and arrived at a solution where both their objectives are met. For example, they could come up with a plan to visit Nisha's town every alternate weekend and on long holidays. That way, both their objectives are met: She won't feel too distanced from her town, and he can get the better paying job and reinstate his family's financial wellbeing.

The question of insecurity usually arises during conversations that are sensitive or awkward in nature. Hence, 9 out of 10 times, the speaker will know that the listener may get uncomfortable and defensive. Thus, following these steps to ensure that the listener feels safe and assured can lead to a successful conversation.

15

Connecting with People

We all would have come across certain people who can talk to just anybody about anything, who can make friends wherever they go, and easily have meaningful conversations with those around them. At new workplaces, they can easily connect with their colleagues and bosses and win their trust.

Whether they are aware of it or not, such people have remarkable communication skills, which they can use to effortlessly form pleasant and agreeable associations with people anywhere. If you have ever found yourself thinking, "I wish I found it just as easy to make friends and talk to people," this chapter can help.

Let us discuss the techniques which will help you develop this skill.

1. **Pay Attention** – The first step to connect with the other person is to pay attention to them, listen to them. We have already discussed the vital importance and many advantages of being a good listener in the earlier part of this book. Listening well alone can help make a deep connection. If possible, try to go beyond the other person's words and grasp the feelings that their words come from. Empathize with those feelings. Use words such as, "I understand…" or "It is but natural for you to feel so…" or "It was natural

for you to act that way..." Very soon, you will observe that people are able to comfortably open up to you and feel safe in confiding in you. It is noteworthy that when you listen to people attentively, they feel connected with you. When they feel connected with you, they become more open to your words when it is your turn to speak. Let us understand more about connecting with emotions better in the next step.

2. **Make them feel positive emotions** – Whether we are aware of it or not, our emotions inspire us more than words. Often, after a long passage of time, we forget the words, but the emotions stay with us. This is because we absorb emotions better than words. Hence, perceiving people on an emotional plane and being empathetic with them helps us connect with them. People who are naturally good at connecting well with people, are able to do so without consciously knowing it. Let us understand this with an example.

Rohan had recently joined his new office and wanted to strike a conversation with Sumeet, whose cubicle was next to his. Once, when he saw that Sumeet wasn't particularly busy, he bent over to his cubicle and said, "Hi Sumeet! May I ask you something if you're not very busy?"

"Sure," replied Sumeet, expecting a question related to work from the newcomer.

"There's a cinema somewhere around here, right? Have you been there?" asked Rohan.

"Sure, I have," replied Sumeet, surprised at the context of the question.

"Nice! Do you remember the first movie you saw there?"

"Hmm... Let me see... I grew up around here, so it was really a long time ago."

"Oh, you grew up around here?! It must be a lovely feeling

to walk the same street you did as a child and see the cinema where you'd seen your first movie!"

Hearing this, Sumeet launched into a feeling of nostalgia, remembering his childhood days. A smile appeared on his lips and he replied, "Yes! Those are memories I cherish..."

Notice how Rohan steered the conversation in such a way as to cause Sumeet to feel a positive emotion. A person's emotions belong in a private space. By making Sumeet feel nostalgic, Rohan stepped over the professional boundary to find the key to Sumeet's private space, thus establishing a connection between them. This gave Rohan a good platform to nurture and grow the relationship further. Sumeet began to feel a connection with Rohan based on this private and positive emotion and warmed up to him.

We considered a workplace example because this technique is especially useful in professional environments where relationships are generally shallow, unemotional, and based on professional needs. An office team, where people are emotionally connected, can function at a higher degree of synergy. People look out and work for each other in a more organic manner without being too self-centered. Such an environment makes people feel comfortable and stress-free. They develop a positive feeling about the company, thus wanting to stay there as long as they can. Most people would give up lucrative job offers to stay in such a congenial and peaceful environment.

It is beneficial for business owners or team leaders to connect with their employees or subordinates on an emotional plane to make them feel relaxed. The purpose here is to make people feel relaxed, not complacent, so that they may work in a stress-free environment which is conducive for higher productivity and satisfaction. For example, a salesperson should feel inspired and motivated by his manager to achieve his targets, not stressed out or pressurized.

Feeling genuine empathy and also expressing it to make people feel better can go a long way in connecting with people.

3. **Find Commonalities** – In addition to paying attention to people and making them feel positive, another way to connect is to find commonalities with them. People who have something in common, get along well. For example, businessmen will get on well with other businessmen. Two people interested in music will connect well.

Having something in common helps us understand people better, which in turn forms a platform for communication. People belonging to similar professions or interests naturally tend to gravitate towards each other. Some people have the natural ability to find commonalities with their audience and connect with them on that basis, but if you are trying to develop this skill, you will need to make it a conscious habit.

Here is one way of doing this. If someone is expressing a problem or describing an incident, something embarrassing for example, it helps if we can quote something similar that has happened to us. Using this common point, we can empathize with them. Our words will carry more meaning too, because the other person will know that we have been through a similar experience.

Amol and Vibha were having a lunch break at work. Vibha had recently joined and was telling Amol her experience about a meeting with her manager, earlier that morning.

"It's so hard to understand him, especially with that accent. Yesterday evening, he asked me to prepare a presentation for today's meeting, but I just couldn't understand what he was saying! I wanted to ask him to repeat, but he was in a hurry and also seemed to be in a foul mood. So, I made the presentation based on whatever I assumed. But it turns out that the presentation was totally off track! I got an earful from him in the meeting today."

"You know, Vibha," replied Amol, "I had the same problem with him when I started working here two years ago. I could never understand what he was saying. But don't worry… you'll get the hang of his accent soon. Meanwhile, whenever you feel in doubt of what he exactly says, instead of asking him to repeat, you can repeat what you've understood. If you're wrong, he will have to explain himself!"

Notice how Amol is able to connect with Vibha by finding a commonality between them. By sharing a similar experience, he made her feel at ease, conveying that she was not the only one to have had such an experience. He also offered her a solution.

Cultivating these three habits will surely get you into the good books of your colleagues, friends, and relatives. People will feel a genuine connection with you, thus enriching the communication to a great extent.

PART 4

THE SIX KEYS TO SUCCESSFUL COMMUNICATION

See People for Who they *Are*, Not Who they *Were*

The past resides only in our memories, the future exists only as our imagination. Meanwhile, the present is here, right now!

"Now" is where awareness is awake, where wakefulness is present; it is where we truly exist. Ideally this is where we should be. Unfortunately, most of the time, we are either consumed by the experiences of the past or the anxieties of the future, or alternating between the two like a pendulum, thus missing out completely on the instantaneous and unadulterated joy in the present.

Naturally, we make the same mistake in our communication too. When we speak to someone, our communication with them is greatly influenced by our past experience with them. In other words, based on our interactions or incidents with them, we form an image or perception about them. The emotions that were aroused during those incidents get locked in our memory. Thereafter, they unconsciously influence our communication with them. In most cases, this continues till the relationship becomes too sour and the two people drift apart completely.

But humans can change every day. We grow and evolve. No perception that is formed of a person today, can be held forever. Hence, it is wrong and also counter-productive to always look at anyone from the lens of our past experiences.

It is possible that the person has now changed and deserves a different response from us. In fact, a different response could even benefit us. Just like a spectacled person cleans his glasses every day, we should clean the glasses of our mental perspective every day and always look afresh at people. Remember that the same applies to us ourselves as well. We may have spoken to someone rudely yesterday because we were in a bad mood or probably because our mind was elsewhere, but that doesn't make us a "rude" person. Speaking angrily, arrogantly, or tauntingly once, doesn't make us an angry, arrogant, or taunting person. We wouldn't want the other person to form that kind of image about us and respond to us accordingly. Likewise, we should give people the same benefit of doubt. We should believe in their ability to change and adapt and give them a fresh look.

Also, whenever engaging in a tricky, sensitive, or emotional conversation—perhaps telling someone about something wrong they've done, or conveying our dissatisfaction about something—we should always resist the urge to say something immediately. We should take a pause, go within. It helps to distance ourselves from the past memories and experiences about that person, anchor ourselves in the present, and then initiate the conversation. This will ensure that our conversation is not shaded by the past. Eventually, the quality of our conversation will be greatly enhanced.

Asking the Right Questions

A restaurant had recently started serving two variants of a particular dish—one with boiled eggs, and one without. After a few weeks, the owner noticed that most of his customers ordered the dish without boiled eggs, due to which too many pre-boiled eggs were wasted.

To find out the reason behind this, he began observing the interaction between the waiters and customers. He noticed that whenever someone would order this dish, the waiters would ask, "And would you like to have it with eggs or without?" The owner got an idea. After closing for the day, he summoned all his waiters and gave them some instructions.

The next day, the chef was surprised to find a sudden rise in the number of dishes that were ordered with boiled eggs. He went to the owner and expressed his surprise and asked what had happened. The owner gave a satisfied smile and said, "Nothing much, I just asked the waiters to change their question. Now they ask, 'And would you like to have it with a single egg or double?'"

"And what if someone doesn't want eggs at all?" asked the curious chef.

"Well, in that case the customer will specifically say that they don't want any eggs, but why give the choice in the first place!?" replied the owner.

It is a human tendency to usually choose "No" when given a choice between "Yes" and "No". The owner had cleverly grasped this fact and changed the options presented to the customers to turn the outcome in his favor. We, too, can often influence the outcome by changing the alternatives we present to our listeners.

Most often, when people ask questions, they present their listeners the alternative of either choosing something or choosing nothing. For example:

"Shall we make dinner together tonight?"

"Shall we clean the house today?"

"Do you think you can handle this new project?"

"Are you going to study at all today?"

"Will you call her and sort things out?"

Observe that to all these questions, the listener can choose to say "No," because it is one of the alternatives offered to them. Studies in human psychology suggest that one would unconsciously prefer to say "No" to anything that is new or outside their comfort zone. If a person has an alternative that will save him from any inconvenience, he will most surely go that way.

In such cases, we can influence the listeners' choice by changing the alternatives we offer. By not giving the choice of nothing or "No", we can restrict the alternatives we offer and make the listener choose between one thing or the other, as against choosing between something and nothing (as in the case of the restaurant). This can also be called the technique of "offering restricted options." For example, the earlier questions can be rephrased as:

"When should we start if we have to make dinner together tonight?"

"With which room do we begin cleaning the house today?"

"By when do you think you can complete this new project? One month or two?"

"When do you plan to study today?"

"Will you be sorting things out with her over the phone, or in person?"

These rephrased questions do not give the listener the alternative of saying "No". This technique is useful with children, especially when parents want to get them to do something that they would otherwise refuse. For example:

"Will you keep your phone aside now, or do you need 5 more minutes with it?"

"Shall we clear your room now or in the evening?"

"Will you have lunch now or after you've finished studying?" (This solicits a positive response for both, lunch and studies)

"Will you have your bath now or after you've played?"

"Will you water the plants before or after breakfast?"

"Shall I get you flavored milk, or would you rather have it plain?"

Thus, the technique of giving restricted options helps us prod children to make desirable choices. Instead of giving a choice of whether they will do something or not, the choice is shifted to how or when they will do it, just by reframing the question.

We can use this technique to save ourselves from looking bad or to save someone from getting hurt as well. Let us consider another example.

Leena had a very demanding manager. One day, he assigned her four priority tasks that would take her the entire next day to complete. By that evening, she had charted an action plan for the next day and was about to leave when she was summoned by her manager again and assigned two more tasks, both of which were critical and had to be completed as soon as possible.

Leena was exasperated. She was now left with two options: either refuse to complete all the six tasks by the next day and risk looking bad; or stretch her working hours the next day and complete all six tasks.

However, she had recently learnt about the technique of giving restricted options, so she requested her manager, "Sir, I had planned to work on the four tasks that you assigned me this morning, all day tomorrow. But as these two tasks are more critical, I will take them up first thing tomorrow morning. About the remaining four tasks, can you please tell me which two of them are on higher priority, so that I can prioritize accordingly and concentrate on completing those in the remaining time tomorrow?"

Leena found a respectful way of communicating that she can complete only four tasks in a day without sounding like she was refusing to work. If the manager wanted her to complete all six tasks on the same day, he may say so specifically. But by tactfully communicating that she can complete only four tasks in a day, she could possibly save herself some trouble.

A word of caution though: When using this technique in a professional environment, one should always be careful of one's responsibilities, authoritative standing, and apply practical sense. For example, one cannot just walk up to one's manager and ask, "Would you give me a pay rise of 30% or 50% this year?!" It would not only sound hilarious but also be inappropriate. Use the technique carefully and only where it is appropriate. Here are some examples.

- The project deadline is approaching, so we all may have to put in some extra hours. Would you prefer to wait after office hours or come on weekends?

- You can hand me the reports in the morning before you start work or in the evenings before you leave. What would you prefer?

- Shall we discuss this now or would you like some time to think?

- Would you like to plan your leaves this month or later during Christmas?

Thus, we have seen how the technique of offering restricted options helps people improve their communication at work, get their children to make the desirable choices, improve their sales, and get a better control on the outcome of their conversations.

Being Respectfully Candid

Earnest Hemingway was an American journalist and writer, who was awarded the Nobel Prize for Literature in October 1954 for his literary works. He was known for his concise and straightforward style of writing.

One of his famous quotes is: "My aim is to put down on paper what I see and what I feel in the best and simplest way." His style of writing is almost a textbook lesson for people who are trying to develop the skills of micro-writing. This skill is especially important for people in the fields of advertising and marketing, for they have to learn to convey a lot in the fewest of words.

One day his son approached him. Having written a story himself, he asked his father to read it and suggest changes to make it sound better. So, Earnest Hemingway read the story written by his son and at the end of it, picked up his pen and made a single change. He scratched out one word and replaced it with another one and gave the pages back to his son.

The son saw that his father had made a single correction and felt disappointed. He thought his father probably hadn't read the whole story or had read it half-heartedly and made some random correction just to get over with it. He asked his father, "Only one correction, father? That too, just one word?!"

"If it is the right one, even a single word should suffice!" replied his father.

This little story illustrates a very important point. Even a single right word that's said or written in the right place and at the right time can have a profound effect. Interestingly, the reverse is equally true. A wrong word in the wrong place or at the wrong time can also have a profound effect! We could spend years explaining a single word that was said in the wrong way, at the wrong time!

Thus, it is important to be respectfully straightforward and not beat around the bush by trying to be too elaborative. When we consciously choose such words that convey the straight and simple meaning in a polite and respectful way, the other ornamental or redundant words automatically fall off. What remains is a condensed and concise essence.

Let us consider two scenarios to understand this further:

Scenario 1: A business owner has a very good and close relationship with one of his employees, perhaps because he has been working with him almost since the inception of the business. However, now the employee's performance has started deteriorating. He has become complacent about his work, which is a great disappointment to the owner. He cannot let this continue without causing serious harm to the well-established business. But at the same time, he hesitates to talk about this sensitive topic to his employee, who is now also a good friend.

Scenario 2: A husband stays busy at work, returns home very late, and plans his weekends with his friends. His wife wants him to spend quality time with their family, but she wants him to realize this on his own without having to pester him about it.

We can imagine many more such scenarios, all of which will have at least one thing in common. In each case, there is a person who finds it difficult to start a conversation about something that is troubling him or her. They are not able to make up their minds about how they should handle the situation. Someone might respond aggressively while someone else might choose to stay silent. But either case would lead to a failure of communication.

Let us first consider the wrong ways of responding in such situations.

Aggressive response – An aggressive response may either come from someone having an aggressive persona or from a passive person who explodes. With such a response, anger and frustration are in the driver's seat. Everything he or she says—whether fact or assumption—comes from anger. In an aggressive response, one compulsively chooses words driven by emotions.

Quite naturally, the listener's focus is entirely on the harsh words that are spoken. The purpose should be to choose words in such a way so as to convey the facts and get the desired outcome, but the very opposite happens.

In Scenario 1 described above, if the boss gives an aggressive response to the underperforming employee-friend, he might say something like, "Do you have any idea how much damage you've caused us in the past six months?! If this continues, I'm sure you will run us all to the ground!"

In Scenario 2, the frustrated wife might say, "You're so irresponsible. You don't care at all about me and our children. Will you ever prioritize your family over your friends?!"

You will notice that both the cases will precipitate into the very opposite of the desired outcome. Thus, getting carried away by emotions leads to failure in communication.

Silent or lukewarm response – Passive people will choose to ignore the problem and postpone confronting it as much as possible. At best, they might express their dissatisfaction in very mild lukewarm words. But the subtlety of their communication will hardly have any impact at all.

For example, in Scenario 1, the boss may choose to ignore the employee's incompetence, postpone the confrontation to such an extent that at one point the entire business gets into risk.

In Scenario 2, the wife may choose to silently continue to tolerate her husband's behavior, every now and then giving a subtle hint about her wishes.

Note that in both the scenarios, a situation will come when the boss or wife will not be able to tolerate any longer and eventually explode, resulting in an aggressive response. Yet again, a communication failure!

Taunting – A taunt or sarcasm is like a shortcut by the speaker to feel a false sense of satisfaction. Let us first consider an example and then discuss this further. In Scenario 2, let's say the wife taunts her husband about his behavior. The conversation runs like this.

Husband: "You know, Paul is getting married!"

Wife: "Oh really?! How nice! I just hope he has honestly told his wife-to-be everything about his lifestyle!"

Husband: "What do you mean 'told her everything'?"

Wife: "Well, about the trips that you friends take every other weekend and your late-night parties. They're getting married. She should know the worst about what she's getting into! I mean it may be too late for some of us, but others can be warned beforehand."

One can almost imagine the awkward silence that follows this conversation. Will this taunt bring the husband and wife any closer? No. On the contrary, such taunts only lead to friction, causing the husband to put even more hours at work, returning home even later than usual.

As mentioned before, taunting someone or indulging in sarcasm is like a shortcut to false satisfaction. Though there is a confrontation, it is indirect. The wife confronts her husband by expressing her feelings indirectly. The listener usually doesn't get a chance to respond to the taunts because the confrontation is indirect. The inability of the listener to respond gives the speaker a sense of satisfaction of having overpowered the other person.

But when people taunt others, they fail to understand that the listener's silence doesn't mean he or she has accepted what they said. Even though the listener may not have said anything, whatever they wanted to say stays suppressed within them and will manifest in some way. If anger is like a hammer that can break relationships, taunting and sarcasm is like rust that corrodes relationships, making them flimsy and brittle. This kills the love, respect, and the feeling of belongingness that is essential in relationships.

Thus, we have seen how the three common responses can lead to communication failure. Let us now look at the fourth response that guarantees success.

Being respectfully candid – The very words "respectfully candid" convey how the communication should be. The very first step when you are trying to start a difficult or awkward conversation is to clean the slate by wiping off negative feelings. This is necessary to make sure your words do not emanate from a negative space.

How can this be done?

One can't wipe out negative emotions by suppressing or resisting them. The way to do that is to observe the emotion as it arises from a detached standpoint and see it dissolve in the ocean of acceptance. Acceptance can dissolve any negative emotion.

In both the scenarios described earlier, if the boss or the wife were to observe their emotions without getting carried away, they would have realized that it was their own avoidance that was building up the frustration and anger within them. Had they communicated with the employee or the husband at the right time in the right way, this could have been avoided. This understanding leads them to the root of their emotion, and then it becomes easy for them to accept what they are feeling.

Dissolving the negative emotion that we have for someone is the foundation for having a respectful conversation. We change the driving emotion from which words emanate. Approaching difficult conversations respectfully allows you to be both objective and empathetic. Thereafter, you need to consider four essential points while speaking.

1. **Respectful words** – Having cleared your negative emotions, the next step is to make sure you use respectful words because you are about to say something that the listener may feel bad about. Consider what you are about to say as a feedback and not a retaliation.

2. **State facts, not accusations or perspectives** – In difficult conversations, it is best to stick to facts instead of blaming or stating your perspectives. The listener may be in a vulnerable state of mind, and your accusations or perspectives may further affect the communication. As facts are irrefutable, they are easier to accept.

   Avoid using accusing words or statements. Rephrase sentences that assign blame to the person. Focus on the intended outcome, not the disappointment.

   In Scenario 1, the boss should stick to facts when discussing the employee's performance—like statistics about the fall in sales, factual reports about degradation of the product quality, or delays in project deliveries, instead of using derogatory words like "incompetent", "irresponsible", "inefficient", "complacent", etc.

   In Scenario 2, the wife should focus on communicating what she would love to see in the relationship rather than how her husband has let her down. She should focus on facts like how she and the family need his time and attention, how his attention for their children is important for their growth, how his continued absence from family matters is distancing him from the family members, etc., instead of calling him irresponsible, careless, or stubborn.

3. **Be calm but solemn** – Stating facts in respectful words needs to be accompanied by a solemn manner of speaking and body language to convey the gravity of the situation. Any visible hesitation or laxness can dilute the seriousness of the situation.

4. **Keep the conversation open ended** – After having conveyed your concerns over the facts in respectful words and a solemn body language, open the conversation to the other person. Let him or her respond to what you have said. Urge them to speak if they don't. Whatever you say should not be intended or even perceived as a judgment to which the person cannot respond. In short, the purpose of the conversation should be to arrive at a solution and not pass judgement.

Let us now revisit the two scenarios in the light of this new understanding.

Scenario 1: Without postponing the awkward conversation, the business owner decides to speak to the employee at an opportune time. He says, "Rohit, what I'm about to tell you is extremely difficult, considering the excellent relationship we share. You have been handling the marketing for southern region for a while now. I must admit that the numbers being reported by your region are far below what you are truly capable of achieving. We must do something soon to reverse this situation or we're risking some serious damage to the business. What do you think we should be doing differently?"

You will notice that this conversation excludes accusations and emotional outbursts. The business owner does express his emotion, but without actually saying it in words. There is no disrespect for the employee anywhere in the conversation. On the contrary, he expresses his confidence in his ability and also states that he values the relationship that they share. The overall progress of the conversation is towards a solution and not to chew on the past.

Scenario 2: The wife confronts her husband one day and tells him, "Girish, I need to talk to you about something very important. I had decided not to say anything about this, but then I also realize that the longer I wait, the worse the situation will become. And I don't want that to happen. I can understand your late working hours on weekdays because I know that work is hectic and your hands are tied there. However, you've been spending the past several weekends with your friends. You need to understand that the weekend is the only opportunity for me and the children to spend quality time with you. We all look forward to it every week. I have already spoken to you about this twice, but you have prioritized your time with friends over your family. So, I want to know if there's something on your mind that is causing you to behave like this? Please tell me if there is anything I should be doing differently."

In this conversation too, you will notice that the wife is not accusing her husband. She is solemnly stating her family's needs and leading the situation towards a solution.

Thus, being respectfully candid can help communicate successfully in difficult and awkward situations.

Sticking to the Topic

Whether it is one-on-one communication or a group discussion, it is commonly observed that conversations tend to drift off topic.

For example, a team meeting is called to discuss a certain issue with an ongoing project, but soon the team is engaged in an animated discussion about how the team lost another project, or how this project is different from other projects that the team had handled in the past. Then someone pulls in everyone's attention to the topic at hand, and everyone circles back to it. But not before a considerable time has been spent discussing everything else but the topic at hand.

One-on-one communication or personal conversations are no exception to this. You may have often had conversations in which you or the other person keeps digressing into other related topics.

Why does this happen?

That's what this chapter is about. We will learn about the tendencies of the mind that cause us to constantly get distracted from the main topic during a conversation. We will also see what we can do to stick to the topic and keep the conversation short yet fruitful.

Let us consider a sample conversation between 4 business partners (A, B, C, and D) who own a company that manufactures an electrical gadget. They have scheduled a meeting to discuss some consumer grievances.

A: Last week I received several mails from consumers who have bought our product X, complaining about its power management function.

B: Yes, I've got similar feedback from many distributors. Customers have been visiting their retailers to complain about the battery.

C: Okay, so we will need to replace all their batteries as per the warranty agreement.

A: Yes, but what if the replacements have the same issue?

B: That's a possibility. Some of the replacement batteries may turn out to be dud as well. The company that we've bought the batteries from does have about 2% to 3% dud batteries per lot. That ratio could go even higher. Choosing them as our vendor may have been a wrong decision.

D: But they were the only company selling us the batteries at an affordable rate. We had to keep the final product cost in check. Choosing this company may have been wrong but it was our only option then.

B: That may be true, but we've compromised too much on quality to keep the cost low. These batteries are ruining our reputation.

D: We can always go for better quality batteries but that will seriously affect our profit margin. We can't afford that. We have no alternative but to keep the product cost low to be able to compete in the market.

A: But we do have alternatives. It's just that we never explored them. Why can't we look at developing and launching new products? Shouldn't we do something in that direction?

D: There are too many challenges with that. Firstly, the R&D in itself will cost us a fortune. Secondly, even if we were to invest in it, the product has to take off well.

C: Having more products in our portfolio will lead to increase in sales. If one product doesn't do well in the market, the other can.

D: You're right, but even if we're able to develop saleable products, we'll have to pour in a lot of money to promote them. So, the R&D cost, the cost of production, distribution, and promotion… There are too many variables!

(…after about 40 minutes of discussion on developing new products…)

A: Guys… One second… We can talk about developing new products later. Right now, we've got to deal with the issue with the existing product. Let's discuss what we can do about the disgruntled customers and what service we can provide to salvage our reputation and save it from getting worse.

Notice how the discussion gets derailed and a lot of productive time is wasted discussing topics that could be taken up later. This example points at the first of the three reasons why discussions go off topic. Let us understand all the three reasons.

Reason 1 – Focus shifts to associated topics

In the above example, when the topic of faulty batteries was initiated, B was reminded of the time when they had decided to tie up with a supplier of batteries, who offered them a cost advantage. Since then, B was skeptical about the substandard quality of batteries that could mar the performance of the final product. The topic at hand refreshes that memory and B brings it to everyone's notice. Note that B did not do this deliberately. It was almost an instant reaction.

In our mind, memories are interconnected. When something particular is mentioned, all the connected memories are invoked. This happens on a subtle level without any conscious intervention on our part. And with the connected memories, come the associated emotions. These emotions can be positive or negative—like the emotion of fear in this example. When the memory and the associated emotion are invoked, we unknowingly get carried away by the emotion and express it in words, and thus the topic shifts. Then someone has to remind us (like 'A' did) of the topic at hand to bring us back to reality.

Going back to the example, B was reminded of the fear and criticized the decision of having chosen the particular supplier for batteries. D, who was in support of the decision, got busy defending the decision. For D, defending the decision became more important than the actual crisis being discussed. And thus, the discussion got derailed. A and C were listening to the two, and A realized that the discussion had got derailed and attempted to bring them back on track, but by then they had already wasted 40 precious minutes.

So, the reason here is the inadvertent shift of interest from the crisis being discussed to some other associated topic that could have been discussed later.

Reason 2 – Lack of ability to multi-switch

When we see people handling multiple tasks at the same time, we call it multi-tasking. It appears that they are getting multiple things done at the same time. But is that really true? Is multi-tasking possible?

No. The human mind is not capable of multi-tasking because it cannot focus on more than one thing at a time. But we do see people doing multiple tasks at the same time. What is that?

That can be called multi-switching. While it is a fact that the mind does not have the ability to focus on more than one thing at the same time, it can be trained to quickly shift focus from one thing to another. So, people who are doing multiple tasks at the same time, are actually switching their focus quickly from one thing to another. Hence the term "multi-switching." Anyone can train their mind and get better at this. The more you practice it, the more you learn to switch between tasks.

To be able to stay on the topic of conversation, one has to develop the skill of multi-switching. It comes in handy when a discussion has to visit many related topics and keep swerving back to the original one. In such conversations, visiting and discussing the related topics is important but it also poses the risk of over-digression from the original topic. The lack of multi-switching can derail a conversation, sometimes even irreversibly.

Reason 3 – Unclear boundaries of conversation

The third reason for derailed conversations is that the boundaries of the conversation are not known or are unclear. This happens particularly in situations where we offer help to someone on some personal matter.

Imagine you are counseling a friend about a problem he or she is facing, and the friend starts listing problems one after the other, forming a long string of miseries. Such a conversation is bound to stray off topic because the boundaries of the conversation have not been decided. Instead of discussing the problem that actually led to the beginning of the conversation, we end up discussing random points that keep coming up—like driving a car without any sense of direction and going whichever way the road takes you.

Let us see how such a conversation might run.

Friend: You know, I'm facing some trouble at work. I'm in a tight situation. Can you guide me on what I should be doing next?

You: Sure, tell me.

Friend: Well, you know I've taken this job recently. My manager is a real workaholic. He expects everyone to put in extra hours just because he refuses to go home on time. I need to make sure I leave by 6 p.m. to collect my daughter from daycare, reach home, and then make dinner. But how can I tell my new boss that I cannot work late?

You: I can understand that you cannot ask for a special treatment especially since you are new at this job. Why don't you tell your husband to manage dinner for a few weeks, while you get well acquainted with your new boss and speak to him about leaving early?

Friend: I can't! My husband says he cannot work in the kitchen. I tried talking to him about it, but things haven't been very smooth between us either.

You: Why? What's happened?

Friend: We've been having arguments too often lately over silly matters. He's been consistently coming home late, even before I started this job when I was at home. We hardly speak to each other these days.

You: That's sad. Why don't you both go for some counselling? I'm sure that will help.

Friend: Well, we've hit a bit of rough patch financially. I had thought about counselling, but we are hardly able to meet the house rent and other expenses. I don't think we can afford professional counselling. I wonder if you could help me out there.

You: Sure, can you both meet me somewhere so we may talk?

Friend: No, I don't think he would agree to come if he knew why we were meeting. And he will surely ask me.

You: Alright, I'll come over to your place and we can talk.

You will observe that the actual point for which the conversation started—helping your friend with a problem at work—remained untouched and the conversation drifted in an altogether different direction. Instead of circling back to the original problem, the conversation wandered away aimlessly and at some point, after the conversation, you are sure to feel that you got involved in your friend's personal matter unknowingly and for no reason.

It is not being said that we shouldn't be offering personal help to friends. However, help should be offered only when we knowingly decide to, not because the conversation you had with your friend lacked boundaries and you unknowingly found yourself in a situation where you couldn't refuse help. At the beginning of the conversation, helping your friend with a personal problem was not your goal. But the actual goal wasn't clearly defined.

Thus, it is important for us to know the boundaries in every relationship, incident, or situation, so that we may communicate accordingly. Not knowing the boundaries can land you in difficult situations every now and then. However, knowing them will alert you as soon as a conversation approaches the boundary and you will instinctively know how to steer the conversation back to the original point.

When you set boundaries before giving advice, motivation, or guidance, you make sure that you stick to the main purpose of the conversation.

Let us consider how the above conversation could proceed in the light of this understanding.

Friend: You know, I'm facing some trouble at work. I'm in a tight situation. Can you guide me on what I should be doing next?

You: Sure, tell me.

Friend: Well, you know I've taken this job recently. My manager is a real workaholic. He expects everyone to put in extra hours just because he refuses to go home on time. I need to make sure I leave by 6 p.m. to collect my daughter from daycare, reach home, and then make dinner. But how can I tell my new boss that I cannot work late?

You: I can understand that you cannot ask for a special treatment especially since you are new at this job. Why don't you tell your husband to manage dinner for a few weeks, while you get well acquainted with your new boss and speak to him about leaving early?

Friend: I can't! My husband says he cannot work in the kitchen. I tried talking to him about it, but things haven't been very smooth between us either.

You: That is sad. I really hope that the two of you are able to work things out. But about your work problem, I think I have an idea. Instead of working late, you can ask your boss if you can start your day early. That way, he won't feel that you are asking for any special treatment, just different working hours. Your husband doesn't want to work in the kitchen, but he can surely drop your daughter to the daycare center.

Friend: Yes, that sounds like a good plan. I'll talk to my boss about it tomorrow and see if he's okay with it. Thank you so much! You've been such a great help!

Notice how in the second instance, knowing the boundaries of the conversation, helps you steer back to the main topic and avoid digression.

Finally, having understood the three reasons why conversations steer off topic, let us understand some important steps that can help us stick to the topic:

1. Before starting any meeting or discussion, clearly state the main point of discussion to the team, group, or to yourself.

2. If there are more than one points of discussion, prepare and present the agenda and ascertain beforehand how much time should be assigned to each topic.

3. If during the meeting, you are reminded of an important topic that also needs to be discussed, write it down and bring it up later instead of interrupting the flow of the meeting. All the participants of the meeting can be given these instructions.

4. If someone shifts to a different topic, patiently hear them out and find out whether what they are talking about is related to the main topic.

    - If it is not related, interrupt them politely, ask them to write down the point and bring it up after the main topic has been addressed.

- If it is related, then employ the skills of multi-switching to make sure the new points do not disrupt the main topic.

5. If a discussion is expected to go off topic, one person can be assigned the responsibility to make sure everyone circles back to the main topic.

6. Define clear boundaries based on your personal and professional relationships and situations.

It is possible that even after taking all these steps, you find that the conversation digresses. When this happens, you can mentally trace back the conversation to the point where it started digressing. You may not be able to trace back every detail to perfection, but the attempt at tracing back will help raise your awareness. This will, in turn, help you stick to the topic in future conversations.

Saying "No"

Your friends are visiting an expensive night club on the weekend. Neither do you have the money to blow off at a night club, nor do you want to indulge. But you are hesitant to say "No" to your friends for the fear of upsetting them.

You have just sat down to study for your exams that are upcoming next week, and you receive a call from a friend who invites you to his birthday party. You want to say "No" but agree to go because he was present at your birthday party. You're afraid that by not going to his, you will disappoint him.

You are already laden with tasks at work and struggling to complete them. A colleague walks up to your desk and requests you to take up one of his tasks because he needs to leave early. You look at the huge pile of files on your desk, but you put on a fake smile and say, "Yes, sure!"

Do any of these scenarios sound familiar?

"No" is such a small word, and yet so much thought and energy goes into saying it! Saying "No" is just as hard as accepting it. Accepting a refusal hurts the ego and saying it stirs up intense negative emotions like guilt and embarrassment. To avoid these, we always say "Yes", even if it is at the cost of our own comfort and ethics. Several famous and influential people consider their ability to say "No" to be an integral part of their success story. Here are some examples.

Josh Billings: "Half of the troubles of life can be traced back to saying 'Yes' too quickly and not saying 'No' soon enough."

Tony Blair: "The art of leadership is saying 'No', not saying 'Yes'. It is very easy to say 'Yes'."

Bill Crawford: "One key to successful relationships is learning to say 'No' without guilt, so that you can say 'Yes' without resentment."

Warren Buffett: "We need to learn the slow 'Yes' and the quick 'No'."

These quotes may sound familiar. You may even have heard other quotes that stress the importance of learning to say "No". Yet, in spite of knowing its importance, many of us find it hard to develop this art. Why is this so?

Let us look at the various possible reasons.

1. **Fear of disappointing or hurting someone** – Whether it is saying "No" to a colleague, to a boss, a friend, relative, spouse or even one's parents, the fear that we might hurt or disappoint them by saying "No" drives us to always say "Yes", whatever be the consequences.

2. **Fear of conflict** – Most of us are scared of inviting a conflict. We dislike others for being angry with us or critical of us. Hence, we avoid saying "No", afraid that it might put us into conflict with someone, whether it is the spouse, a friend, or a boss. Many parents avoid refusing their children, because they feel that if they were to say "No" to them, they would stop loving them.

   Our childhood is fraught with lessons about not going against authority. We are supposed to do what our parents, teachers, and others in a position of authority tell us to do. We obey them not only out of the fear of being punished but also because of a deep desire to please them and be loved by these people whom we consider very important. This worry is carried by us into adulthood. We feel an intense desire to fit in with and be liked by our peers.

Research has shown that everyone has a tremendous need to belong to a peer group. Boy or girl, man or woman, we desire acceptance and approval by our friends and relatives. We derive our sense of identity from the fulfilment of this desire. Hence, we feel uncomfortable about entering into conflict and falling out of such a group.

3. **Failure in recognizing the extent of commitment** – Sometimes, we say "Yes" without knowing or understanding the full impact of saying "Yes". This can happen at the workplace or at home. You take on things that, on the face of it, look super easy, but which turn out to be far more complicated than you ever imagined. It is only later that you realize the impact that agreement will have on the rest of your day, week, or month.

4. **Fear of being perceived as someone who is difficult to get along with** – It is possible that your likes and dislikes are very different from your colleagues or friends. You like jazz while they like rock. You like a quiet evening by the riverside while they prefer to visit the club across the city. You like vintage movies while they like the latest action thrillers. So, when a night out is planned, you know that it will be all about going to the club, hearing loud rock music, or a late-night action thriller fest. But you still say "Yes" because you're afraid you might be looked upon as someone who doesn't get along.

5. **The need to prove your worth** – If a person is suffering from low self-esteem or feels insecure about his or her job, then that person might be inclined to always say "Yes". This comes from a deep-seated desire to prove one's worth. Saying "No" is perceived as a weakness or a proof of

incompetence. If the circumstances were any different or if the person felt better about himself, he'd probably have the courage and wisdom to say "No".

With this knowledge, we need to think before we accept any request each and every time. In addition to the reasons listed here, we need to be absolutely certain that what we're taking on is a good idea. After all, it's much harder to get out of something later than turning it down in the beginning.

What can be done to develop the art of saying "No"?

1. Practice saying "No" in small trivial situations like buying something at a mall or store.
2. Take a pause before you say "Yes" or "No", thus giving yourself a space in which you can quickly assess the implications of your response.
3. Take a minute to analyze how bad the negative emotions (guilt, anxiety, or disappointment) will be if you were to say "No". Would you be able to tolerate them? Is it worth doing it, so as to not have those feelings?
4. Analyze the physical implications of saying "No". Are they really as bad as you think they would be? Again, is it worth doing what you are being asked to do to avoid the implications?

Here are some examples of how we can respectfully say "No" in various everyday scenarios.

- Please give me some time to think about this. I will reply on this soon.
- If I take up this new task, I won't have sufficient time to complete the other two tasks.
- I won't be able to participate in your program, but I can help you publish it on the blog.

- Thanks for considering me, but looking at my workstack, I feel I won't be able to make it.

- I have promised my family that I will try and balance my life at work and home. Hence, I won't be able to do justice to this new project.

- Thank you so much for your kind invitation, but my son will need me on that day as he is playing his final match in the annual school championship.

- Sorry, I cannot commit right now. If I find time, I will surely try to take this task later.

- If I take up this one additional responsibility, I would be upsetting my family.

- I would really love to help you out, but I'm not sure whether I can find the time for it.

- I wouldn't like to say "No", but I can't say "Yes" either.

- I don't think I would be the right person to give you an opinion on this subject.

Finally, remember that the art of saying "No" should not be used as a way to weasel out of commitments or responsibilities. In many cases, "Yes" could be the more appropriate and beneficial answer.

Having Difficult Conversations Gracefully

In this chapter, we will discuss the common mistakes we make while having a difficult or awkward conversation, thus causing communication failure. But before we dive into that, let us take a quick look at some situations that can be categorized as "difficult" or "awkward" conversations.

- A conversation in which we are planning to give someone negative feedback and are expecting the listener to get provoked in defense.

- A conversation during which you arrive at a particular point when you realize that your views are completely opposing the other person's views.

- When you and the other person want different outcomes from a conversation.

- During a discussion on emotional topics, like parents discussing issues about their children.

- A conversation in which you are discussing a topic which you know is going to have a profound financial, social, or mental impact on the listener. For example, informing someone that he has been fired.

- A conversation in which the listener is already unhappy or frustrated and is likely to take it out on you.

Many of us will find at least one of the above conversations similar to what we have experienced in our life. All these are conversations in which the situation can get very awkward and we need to be well prepared to handle the challenge. It is possible that during the conversation, you or the other person may say something unpleasant that neither of you would like to hear. Hence, plan to have such conversations when there is no one around.

Let us now understand the common mistakes and how they can be avoided during difficult conversations.

1. **Prepare beforehand**

    Usually, people prepare for a conversation by repeating what they intend to say in their mind. However, trying to do this in a stressful situation can lead to a chaotic state of mind, that will be difficult to overcome. People may end up overthinking and obsessing over the conversation for hours on end. This does more harm than good.

    Instead, we should determine beforehand how much time we are going to assign for the preparation. Tell yourself, "I will give this preparation not more than half an hour, after which I will continue my other tasks." During the assigned half hour, make sure you do nothing but contemplate and prepare for the conversation based on facts and logic. When the conversation actually begins, stay flexible to adapt to the situation and make necessary changes to your talk track.

    Following questions will help prepare for the conversation in the predetermined time interval you have assigned to it:

    - Conversational Goal

        What is the outcome you are expecting from the conversation? Are there any subconscious expectations that have not been brought to light? Sit with yourself for a little while and scour the depth of your mind to find out if there are any unknown expectations. Secondly, try to think of what the other person might be expecting from the conversation too. Bringing these things to light is very important to get a perspective on the likely direction of the conversation. Unless the goals of both parties are clear, it will be impossible to arrive at a common goal.

- Assumptions and Preconceived notions

Try to find out if the other person is holding some assumption about you or your situation in their mind. If yes, these assumptions can lead to miscommunication and misunderstandings during the conversation. Knowing the assumptions beforehand will help you clear any misunderstandings before they take deep roots.

If these false assumptions are causing the other person to feel less secure during the conversation, clearing them can restore their feeling of security. Also find out whether you are harboring any false assumptions or perceptions about the other person. If any, clear them out so that you may approach the conversation with a clean slate and no biases against the person.

- Attitude and Manner

Find out the attitude and manner in which you and the other person will be approaching the conversation. For example, let's say that you know that the other person is aggressive, and you are passive. So, during the conversation it is possible that the other person's words and body language may get aggressive. In such a scenario, all your attention will naturally focus on his harsh words and body language and you may tend to oppose or reject his ideas, even though they may be relevant and appropriate. Think of all such situations that can arise due to the attitude and manner of both parties to avoid such communication failures.

- Finding Common Ground

    If you know that the conversation will throw up opposing expectations, contemplate beforehand about what objections both of you may have for each other's expectations. When you are aware of the other person's objections to your expectations, it becomes easier to discuss and arrive at a common middle path.

2. **Begin by meditating**

    If possible, be in meditation at least for a few minutes before you begin the conversation. Meditation helps calm down the chaos and clutter in the mind and improves the connection between the mind and the heart. Meditating is like taking a quick dip in the lake of inner tranquility. Observe whatever thoughts are going through your mind at the time. Watching our thoughts like we watch a movie, reduces the power of stray thoughts, reducing their impact on our clarity. It serves the purpose of calming the mind like the calming of the ripples on the surface of agitated waters.

3. **Make the right start**

    Beginning a difficult conversation is what most of us dread the most. So much that we keep postponing it till it becomes too late and the situation worsens, causing a lot of trauma and losses to both the sides. Following are some examples that will help as appropriate starters to the conversation:

    - I know we feel very differently about _____. I want to understand what you think and feel about it.

    - I sincerely want both of us to come to some common understanding about _____. I want to understand your thoughts and feelings and also share my own with you. I hope this is fine.

    - I want to talk to you about _____. I know we have opposing views about it, but I am hoping our conversation will help us come to some kind of a common understanding.

These sentences can help start the conversation on the right note.

4. Consult the plan, but you need not stick to it

If you have followed all the steps until now, you will have a plan in your mind about how you want the conversation to proceed. Having a plan for communication is a good practice but sticking rigidly to it is not. During the conversation, you may come across several new points that are relevant to the topic being discussed, which you hadn't thought about while chalking out your plan. You have to keep an open heart and an open mind to incorporate these new developments in the conversation and make impromptu changes.

5. Create a balance of logic and emotions

Some people always prioritize logic over emotions in their arguments, while others do the exact opposite. But as the Greeks put it, "Great messages are composed of both logos and pathos: content and passion." We have to strike a balance between logic and emotions. There are things that one can do that the other can't, so both of them are important. If you are predominantly logical, you may not experience strong emotional surges, but you can verbalize your emotions by saying things like:

"I can see that you are very disappointed by this _____," or,

"I want you to know that _____ has made me feel sorrowful."

On the other hand, if you are predominantly emotional, you will never have problems expressing your emotions verbally or otherwise, but you can make use of lists to put forth logical points well.

6. Be prepared for more than one meeting

Often people expect matters to be wrapped up in a single meeting, which can turn out to be an impractical expectation. They prepare for a single meeting and in a hurry to wrap things up, they often overlook important points and facts that come up. The conversation soon starts slipping out of their hands and they feel agitated. In their haste, they end up saying something that could cause irreversible damage to the conversation. Hence, we should be open to having multiple conversations or meetings even if we hadn't expected that in the first place. We need not hesitate in saying, "No problem… We can always circle back to this matter in the next meeting."

7. Give others a chance to speak and listen carefully

People usually insist on being heard before anything else. Giving your own opinions and perspectives priority over everyone else's, makes others feel mistreated and insecure during the conversation. We have already discussed the importance of becoming better listeners, so we know that we have to give everyone a chance to speak and be heard. The more you listen to others, the more they are likely to listen to you—plain and simple!

8. Always remember the common goal

After having negotiated and arrived at a common goal, it is important to drive the discussion towards that common goal. Conversations often digress into other matters that come up during discussions and valuable time gets wasted. To avoid this, always keep an eye on the common goal. Write it down on paper or on a whiteboard if possible so that everyone can see it all the time. Additionally, have faith that common goals can be met. It is possible to arrive at win-win situations where all parties benefit mutually. Verbalize this faith as many times as possible to make everyone feel the same.

9. Don't make the problem personal

In a discussion, one person cannot dictate to others. A discussion is a two-way interaction. When we go to the depth of a certain subject or become experts at it, we often get strongly attached to our perspectives and opinions about it. So much that any rejection or even the slightest opposition to our opinions makes us take things too personally. Consequently, the main topic of discussion gets brushed aside and we end up putting all our energy into defending and justifying ourselves. If we find ourselves taking things personally, we should remind ourselves of the real purpose of the discussion.

Thus, carefully studying these nine points can help you prepare and carry out any difficult or awkward conversation, whether personal or professional.

Saying the Unsaid

Once, there lived a poor woodcutter. He would walk to the nearby forest every morning, spend the day cutting down trees, and would sell the chopped wood in the market in the evenings. Such was his daily schedule for earning his bread and butter. On his way to the forest and back, he would pass the king's palace. The king would gaze out of the terrace and catch sight of the woodcutter passing by the palace gates.

Every time the king saw the woodcutter, he felt an intense dislike for him. The king was surprised at how he felt so strongly about the innocent passerby. He pondered, "I know I should feel pity for this poor woodcutter, and yet I feel intense hatred. What could be the reason?!" He tried to analyze his feelings but found no answer. No matter how cheerful and pleasant the king felt before he saw the woodcutter, as soon as he saw him, his emotions would change.

One fine day, he decided to discuss this matter with one of his ministers—the wisest among them. He summoned the minister and told him about the woodcutter who passed by the palace gate every day and how he felt intense hatred towards him. The minister knew the king to be a very just, generous, and kind ruler, so even he was surprised at this revelation. However, he assured the king that he would get to the bottom of the matter and report back to him with his findings.

The minister employed his servant to find out the poor woodcutter's name and where he lived. After having found all that, he disguised himself as a common trader and visited the woodcutter. It was as humble a home as a poor worker can be expected to have. The woodcutter welcomed the trader with as much hospitality as he could extend and the two sat down to talk.

After a long conversation with the woodcutter, all the minister was able to find out was that he was just a common worker, who did nothing much other than his menial job every day to be able to afford the bare necessities for his livelihood. Finally, disappointed by the futility of his visit, the minister rose to leave. However, just before he could step out of the woodcutter's house, he noticed a locked door. Pointing at the locked door, he asked the woodcutter. "Why do you keep that door locked?"

"That room," replied the woodcutter, "holds the key to my prosperity!"

Intrigued by the answer, the minister asked the woodcutter what he meant. The woodcutter rushed inside to get the key, unlocked the door, and held the door open for the minister to look inside. The minister was surprised to see the room filled with chopped pieces of wood, neatly arranged in a pile.

"What is all this?!" he asked the woodcutter.

"This is sandalwood," replied the woodcutter with a smile. "I've been collecting it for a long time now."

"It can fetch a good price in the market. Why are you collecting it instead of selling it?" asked the minister.

The woodcutter grinned, "When our king dies, he will need firewood for the royal cremation. I will offer all this sandalwood and get the best price on that day! I pass the palace gates every day wondering about the king's health. The day the king dies, my life will take a turn for the better!"

The minister smiled, having found a satisfactory answer to his question and also achieved the purpose of his visit. He told the woodcutter, "There is still a long time for the king to die, but I have a better idea. The king's son will soon be returning home after his education. Why don't you offer the king this sandalwood to embellish his son's quarters? I've heard that the king is very kind and generous. I'm sure he will reward you handsomely, and you won't have to wait for him to die!"

Saying thus the minister left. A few weeks later, the king summoned the minister again.

"Do you remember I'd told you about that woodcutter a few weeks ago and how I felt an unexplained hatred towards him? Surprisingly, I haven't been feeling the same way about him since the last few days! I've noticed that my feelings for him have undergone a drastic change. Now I actually feel compassionate for him! I don't understand this."

At that point, the minister told the king about his conversation with the woodcutter. The whole thing suddenly made complete sense to the king and he could now see the cause of his original feeling of hatred and why it had undergone a change.

This story illustrates a very important secret about our subconscious mind. Communication between two people begins on a subconscious level long before they speak or even meet each other. Communication occurs on two levels—conscious and subconscious. Conscious communication is the easier one to perceive for obvious reasons, but not the subconscious one.

However, those who are acutely sensitive or who have trained themselves to be receptive to subtle communication, will be able to grasp subconscious communication as well. You may have seen people who have a natural instinct about whether they should trust a person or not. It is said that women in particular have this inborn instinct. This comes from their understanding of the subconscious communication from the other person.

It has been scientifically proven that when people communicate with each other, verbal communication contributes only about 7% whereas the remaining 93% comes from body language, facial expression, and voice modulation. The numbers may vary for different tests, but the fact remains undisputed—that the subconscious mind has more control over our body language, facial expression, and voice modulation. The control of the conscious mind is mostly limited to words and logic. So, if we have hatred or jealousy in our mind for someone, we will consciously sugarcoat our words, but the body language, facial expression, and voice modulation may not be able to completely disguise our true feelings while we speak to them. Not only does our subconscious mind communicate with the other person's subconscious mind, but also influences a majority of our own communication.

For this reason, when appreciating someone, it is said that one should refrain from indulging in excessive or fake flattery because the subconscious mind will surely communicate the truth and we will lose our credibility. This principle is applicable to all the cases where one's words and feelings are not aligned.

Thus, to become better communicators, it is very important for us to work on the inner element of emotions and feelings as much as we work on the outer elements discussed in the earlier parts of this book. The most direct way of changing our emotions is by changing our self-talk. Our self-talk has a direct effect on our emotions and our emotions, in turn, constantly influence our self-talk. The two always complement each other, thus completing the circle.

Self-talk, as the term suggests, is the constant talking that our mind does within. It is the voice of the mind that is always busy commenting, judging, labelling, comparing, and analyzing things. Self-talk is also the beliefs that we verbalize, like:

"The world is a bad place and people are mean."

"This person is so selfish; I hate him."

"I am not capable of doing this."

Here is a very relevant example of the effects of self-talk, taken from the book titled "The Inner Magic" authored by Sirshree.

A disciple once confessed to his Guru that he was frustrated. On being asked the reason, he told, "I'm frustrated with my boss. For many years now, he has been mean and unjust to me. I have always tried to live up to his expectations, but he always finds fault with my work and humiliates me in front of my colleagues. He always assigns me tasks that are not a part of my job description and I don't have the necessary skills to do them. Then he expects me to pull a miracle and complete them to perfection. I am done with this job! I am going to resign tomorrow. I will slam my resignation letter on his desk, clear my financial dues, and be done with it by the end of the day!"

The Guru heard him out patiently and at the end of his clamor, he spoke, "You feel like resigning this job. That is fine, but consider waiting for fifteen days before you do that."

"Why is that?!" asked the surprised disciple.

"Because I want you to do a little experiment for fifteen days, at the end of which you are free to resign the job. All you have to do for these fifteen days is pray twice a day." said the Guru.

"Okay," said the disciple, still confused. "And what am I to pray for?"

"You have to pray for your boss," said the Guru. "You have to pray for the fulfilment of all his wishes and dreams. You have to wish for his good health and prosperity, and for his wellbeing and harmony in his family."

"No way!" said the disciple, turning indignant, "Why should I pray for him, of all the people?!"

"Look, you have already made up your mind about resigning the job, right? Then it hardly matters whether you do it now or after fifteen days. And with regards to praying for him, just do it because I say so."

"Alright, I will do it only because you are saying so…" said the disciple, trying to sound convinced, "but to what end?"

"That, we will discuss when we meet next. For now, all you have to do is pray twice a day for fifteen days, that's all," said the Guru, wrapping up the conversation.

Fifteen days later, when the disciple came back to the Guru, he looked less agitated than before and even had a little smile on his face.

"So, tell me," said the Guru, "all set to resign?"

"I'm confused," replied the disciple still smiling, "Two weeks ago, when I met you, I was so sure that I wanted to resign, but I'm not able to make up my mind about it anymore."

"Why do you think so?" asked the Guru.

"Well, ever since I've started praying for him, there has been a gradual positive change in the way my boss' demeanor! He smiles when he talks to me now. He even appreciated me during the meeting yesterday. He has also started cutting me some slack about the deadlines he gives for my tasks. I just don't understand how this has happened. It's like a miracle!"

"Don't you see what happened?" replied the Guru smiling. "When you started praying for your boss, your self-talk about him changed and that immediately changed your emotions for him! The change in your emotions not only brought about a change in your voice and manner of speaking, but also in your body language. Even if you do not verbalize whatever you feel about a person, it gets communicated to him on the level of the subconscious mind.

"When you were harboring extreme hatred for him, that was being communicated to him by your subconscious mind. Now that you have changed your emotions for him, that is being communicated too! Your subconscious mind cannot harbor negative thoughts for someone who you pray for twice a day! It is bound to feel positive about him and this positivity gets communicated to his subconscious mind. Then he begins to reciprocate. Do you now understand why you were asked to pray for him?!"

"Yes, I now understand, O wise one!" said the disciple, with a wider smile.

This example illustrates how prayers and positive self-talk can change the way we feel about someone or something on a subconscious level. This change brings about a change in our body language, voice, and facial expressions—all of which are communicated to the other person's subconscious mind, whether we want it or not. Hence, by making preparations on our subconscious level, the chances of having a successful conversation and a successful relationship with someone are greatly enhanced.

Let us now take a look at the action plan to prepare ourselves on a subconscious level. Let's say there is someone in our life, with whom we need to have a delicate or sensitive conversation. It could be an arrogant or demanding client, or a smug relative, and we do not feel positively about that person. Here are three steps we need to take to prepare ourselves for the conversation.

Step 1 – Pray for the person

This may sound easier said than done, especially if our emotions are intensely negative. We may feel a strong resistance from within to pray for such a person. But here's the interesting part: the resistance we feel is itself the greatest proof of how important and urgent it is for us to pray for the person and change how we feel about him or her! The prayer can be as follows:

> "May God bless you with good health, happiness, and prosperity. May all your wishes come true. May you be cured of all illnesses and be immune to any health hazards. May your relationships grow stronger. May you evolve holistically and be blessed with a life of peace and completeness!"

Step 2 – Forgive and seek forgiveness

In this very important and crucial step, we honestly and open heartedly ask for the person's forgiveness for any hurt we may have knowingly or unknowingly caused them. Even if the person doesn't actually see or hear us asking for forgiveness, be rest assured that our plea does reach their subconscious mind. Also, asking for forgiveness cleanses and purifies our own heart and mind. To do this, you can close your eyes, imagine the person standing before you, and pray:

> "In the presence of God Almighty, I would like to ask you to please forgive me for any hurt I may have caused you, knowingly or unknowingly, through my feelings, thoughts, speech, or actions. I too forgive you for any hurt that you may have caused me, knowingly or unknowingly, through your feelings, thoughts, words, or actions. Please know that I harbor no ill-will towards you. I wish that you to release yourself from any ill-will you may be feeling for me!"

Whenever possible, ask for forgiveness in person as that is definitely more effective. But in cases where we feel hesitant to face the other person, or if the other person is hesitant to face us, or in any other case where direct communication is not possible for any reason, we can seek forgiveness in the indirect way described above.

Step 3 – Initiate subjective communication beforehand

Choose a time when the other person is expected to be in a relaxed state of mind—late nights or early mornings should be appropriate. During these times, chances are that the other person may not be doing anything important and is in a more relaxed and receptive state of mind.

Close your eyes, imagine the person in front of you and speak to them. If you expect the person to be angry, request them to calm down. Tell them in your mind:

> "Please calm down. I am sure we will find a way out of this situation. I have let go of all my negative feelings for you and I request you to do the same. I truly respect you and want you to be a positive part of my life. I wish you well in all facets of your life."

After having said this, come to the main topic of conversation and begin telling them whatever you feel about it.

After practicing the three steps of prayer, forgiveness, and subjective communication for a few days, when we will actually begin the conversation, we will observe a noticeable change in the person's behavior and responses. It is possible that the other person might feel surprised too, because they are unaware of the communication that has taken place on the subconscious level!

Practice these three steps patiently and persistently with your family, friends, colleagues, and neighbors, and you will begin to experience a miraculous transformation in the quality of your relationships!

Self-Review through Introspection

Having read all the chapters of this book, we can now review, recollect, and reflect on what we have gathered. For this, we will spend some time introspecting on how we can apply what we have read and understood.

The following questions will serve as guidelines for this introspection. Take each question and write down your contemplation in a diary or a journal, which can serve as a ready reference.

1. What are the causes for miscommunication and misunderstanding that I have experienced in my life? What will I do to overcome such instances in the future?

2. What steps will I take to improve my listening skills in the specific conversations in my daily life?

3. How will I put my words to the right use?

4. In which scenarios do I need to express empathy, genuine appreciation, and gentleness?

5. What are the points that I will remind myself before criticizing anyone?

6. What are the specific situations that I face, in which I will *critiguide* instead of criticizing people?

7. Which words of mine tend to hurt the self-image of others? Henceforth, how can I change my words, so as to safeguard others' self-image?

8. How is the communication platform in my family? What steps can I take to improve it?

9. In which relationships do I experience a glass wall? What steps will I take to break this wall?

10. What safeguard words will I introduce in my speech to give a safe and comfortable feeling to specific people with whom I interact?

11. What techniques will I put to practice to create a sense of connectedness in my conversations with others?

12. Where and how will I apply the technique of asking the right questions?

13. In which scenarios do I need to apply the "Respectfully Candid" technique of communication?

14. During which conversations do we tend to drift from the main topic? How will I apply the "Stick to the topic" technique in these cases?

15. In which scenarios do I hesitate to say "No"? Henceforth, which techniques will I use to say "No" in these scenarios?

16. Which techniques given in this book will I remember and apply to handle difficult conversations? How will I prevent

conversations from getting derailed, and how will I salvage strained conversations?

17. How will I implement the technique of "Saying the unsaid"?

• • •

You can send your opinion or feedback on this book to:
Tej Gyan Foundation, P.O. Box 25, Pimpri Colony,
Pimpri, Pune – 411017, Maharashtra, INDIA
Email: englishbooks@tejgyan.org

About Sirshree

Sirshree's spiritual quest, which began during his childhood, led him on a journey through various schools of thought and prevalent meditation practices. His overpowering desire to attain the Truth made him relinquish his teaching profession. After a long period of contemplation on the truth of life, his spiritual quest culminated in the attainment of the ultimate truth. Since then, over the last two decades, he has dedicated his life toward elevating mass consciousness and making spiritual pursuit simple and accessible to all.

Sirshree espouses, **"All paths that lead to the truth begin differently, but culminate at the same point – understanding. Understanding is complete in itself. Listening to this understanding is enough to attain the truth."**

Sirshree has delivered more than 3000 discourses that throw light on this understanding, simplify various aspects of life and unravel missing links in spirituality. He delivers the understanding in casual contemporary language by weaving profound aspects into analogies, parables and humor that provoke one to contemplate.

To make it possible for people from all walks of life to directly experience this understanding, Sirshree has designed the *Maha Aasmani Param Gyan Shivir* – a retreat designed as a comprehensive system for imparting wisdom. This system for wisdom, which has been accredited with ISO 9001:2015 certification, has inspired thousands of seekers from all walks of life to progress on their journey of the Truth. This system makes the wisdom accessible to every human being, regardless of religion, caste, social strata, country or belief system.

Sirshree is the founder of Tej Gyan Foundation, a no-profit organization committed to raising mass consciousness with branches in India, the United States, Europe and Asia-Pacific. Sirshree's retreats have transformed the lives of thousands and his teachings have inspired various social initiatives for raising global consciousness.

His published work includes more than 100 books, some of which have been translated in more than 10 languages and published by leading publishers. Sirshree's books provide profound and practical reading on existential subjects like emotional maturity, harmony in relationships, developing self-belief, overcoming stress and anxiety, and dealing with the question of life-beyond-death, to name a few. His literature on core spirituality expounds the deeper meaning of self-realization and self-stabilization, unravelling missing links in the understanding of karma, wisdom, devotion, meditation and consciousness.

Various luminaries and celebrities like His Holiness the Dalai Lama, publishers Mr. Reid Tracy, Ms. Tami Simon and Yoga Master Dr. B. K. S. Iyengar have released Sirshree's books and lauded his work. "The Source" book series, authored by Sirshree, has sold over 10 million copies in 5 years. His book, "The Warrior's Mirror", published by Penguin, was featured in the Limca Book of Records for being released on the same day in 11 languages.

About 'Happy Thoughts Initiative'

'Happy Thoughts Initiative' is an imprint of WOW Publishings. The publications bearing this imprint are aimed at improving the quality of life in a changing world, so as to raise the level of consciousness and create a progressive society. This is achieved by bringing together researched matter on various facets of life transformation and mind science that align with the philosophy of Tejgyan Global Foundation.

Publications of 'Happy Thoughts Initiative', are available in print and online as books, articles and audibles in English and Hindi. They help in inspiring readers from all walks of life to achieve transformation in the five planes of life viz. Physical, Emotional, Social, Financial and Spiritual.

Tejgyan... The Road Ahead
What is Tejgyan?

Tejgyan is the wisdom of the existential truth, which is beyond duality. "Gyan" is a term commonly used for "knowledge". Tejgyan is the wisdom beyond knowledge and ignorance. It is understanding that arises from direct experience of the final truth. It is what sets us free from the limitations of the mind and opens us to our highest potential.

In today's world, there are people who feel disharmony and are desperately trying to achieve balance in an unpredictable life. Tejgyan helps them in harmonizing with their true nature, the Self, thereby restoring balance in all aspects of their lives.

And then, there are those who are successful, but feel a sense of emptiness within. Tejgyan provides them fulfilment and helps them to embark on a journey towards self-realization. There are others who feel lost and are seeking the meaning of life. Tejgyan helps them to realize the true purpose of human life.

All this is possible with Tejgyan due to a very simple reason. The experience of the ultimate truth (God or Pure consciousness) is always available. The direct experience of this truth is possible provided the right method is known. Tejgyan is that method, that understanding.

The understanding of Tejgyan makes it possible to lead a life of freedom from fear, worry, anger and stress. It helps in attaining physical vitality, emotional strength and stability, harmony in relationships, financial freedom and spiritual progress.

At Tej Gyan Foundation, Sirshree imparts this understanding through a System for Wisdom – a series of retreats that guides participants step by step towards realizing the true Self, being established in the experience of self-realization, and expressing its qualities. This system for wisdom has been accredited with the ISO 9001:2015 certification.

Maha Aasmani Param Gyan Shivir

"**Maha Aasmani Param Gyan Shivir**" is the flagship Self-realization retreat offered by Tej Gyan Foundation. The retreat is conducted in Hindi. The teachings of the retreat are non-denominational (secular).

This residential retreat is held for 3 to 5 days at the foundation's MaNaN Ashram amidst the glory of the mountains and the pristine beauty of nature. The Ashram is located at the outskirts of the city of Pune in India, and is well connected by air, road and rail. The retreat is also held at other centres of Tej Gyan Foundation across the world.

You can participate in this retreat to attain ageless wisdom through a unique System for Wisdom so that you can:

1. Discover "Who am I" through direct experience.
2. Learn to abide in pure consciousness while functioning in the world, allowing the qualities of consciousness like peace, love, joy, compassion, abundance and creativity to manifest.
3. Acquire simple tools to use in everyday life, which help quiet the chattering mind.
4. Get practical techniques to be in the present and connect to the source of all answers within (the inner guru).
5. Discover missing links in the practices of Meditation (*Dhyana*), Action (*Karma*), Wisdom (*Gyana*) and Devotion (*Bhakti*).
6. Understand the nature of your body-mind mechanism to attain freedom form its tendencies.
7. Learn practical methods to shift from mind-centered living to consciousness-centered living.

A Mini-retreat is also conducted, especially for teenagers (14 to 16 years of age) during summer and winter vacations.

To register for retreats, visit www.tejgyan.org,

contact (+91) 9921008060, or email mail@tejgyan.com

About Tej Gyan Foundation

Tej Gyan Foundation (TGF) was established with the mission of creating a highly evolved society through all-round development of every individual that transforms all the facets of their lives. It is a non-profit organization, founded on the teachings of Sirshree.

The Foundation has received the ISO certification (ISO 9001:2015) for its system of imparting wisdom. It has centres all across India as well as in other countries. The motto of Tej Gyan Foundation is 'Happy Thoughts'.

At the core of the philosophy of Tejgyan is the Power of Acceptance. Acceptance has profound meaning and is at the core of our Being. It is Acceptance that brings forth true love, joy and peace.

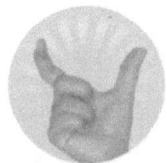

Symbol of Acceptance

The Symbol of Acceptance – shown above – is a representation of this truth. The symbol represents brackets. Whatever occurs in life falls within these brackets that signify acceptance of whatever is. Hence, this symbol forms the centerpiece of the Foundation's MaNaN Ashram.

The Foundation is creating a highly evolved society through:

- Tejgyan Programs (Retreats, YouTube Webcasts)
- Tejgyan Books and Apps
- Tejgyan Projects (Value education, Women empowerment, Peace initiatives)

The Foundation undertakes projects to elevate the level of consciousness among students, youth, women, senior citizens, teachers, doctors, leaders, professionals, corporate and Government organizations, police force, prisoners etc.

Good News!

Maha Aasmani Param Gyan Retreat
is now conducted ONLINE in Hindi!

You can participate in the retreat from the convenience of your home. The retreat is conducted in 3 parts during weekends:

1. The Foundation Truth retreat

2. The Bright Responsibility retreat

3. The Maha Aasmani final retreat

For more details, please call: +91 9921008060, +91 9921008075

To register, visit: https://www.tejgyanglobal.org/mareg

Books can be delivered at your doorstep by registered post or courier. You can request the same through postal money order or pay by VPP. Please send the money order to either of the following two addresses:

WOW Publishings Pvt. Ltd.

1. Registered Office: E-4, Vaibhav Nagar, Near Tapovan Mandir, Pimpri, Pune - 411017.

2. Post Box No. 36, Pimpri Colony Post Office, Pimpri, Pune - 411017

Phone No: (+91) 9011013210 / 9623457873

You can also order your copy at the online store:

www.gethappythoughts.org

*Free Shipping plus 10% Discount on purchases above Rs. 500/-

SELECT BOOKS AUTHORED BY SIRSHREE

   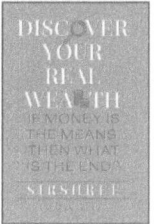
 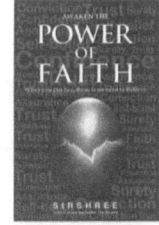  

To order these and other books authored by Sirshree
Visit **www.gethappythoughts.org**

For further details contact:

Tejgyan Global Foundation

Registered Office:

Happy Thoughts Building, Vikrant Complex, Near Tapovan Mandir, Pimpri, Pune 411017, Maharashtra, India.
Contact No: 020-27411240, 27412576
Email: mail@tejgyan.com

MaNaN Ashram:

Survey No. 43, Sanas Nagar, Nandoshi gaon, Kirkatwadi Phata, Sinhagad Road, Tal. Haveli, Dist. Pune 411024, Maharashtra, India.

Contact No: 992100 8060.

Hyderabad: 9885558100, Bangalore: 9880412588,

Delhi : 9891059875, Nashik: 9326967980, Mumbai: 9373440985

For accessing our unique 'System for Wisdom' from self-help to self-realization, please follow us on:

	Website Online Shopping/ Blog	www.tejgyan.org www.gethappythoughts.org
twitter	Video Channel	www.youtube.com/tejgyan For Q&A videos: http://goo.gl/YA81DQ
facebook	Social networking	www.facebook.com/tejgyan
twitter	Social networking	www.twitter.com/sirshree
	Internet Radio	http://www.tejgyan.org/internetradio.aspx

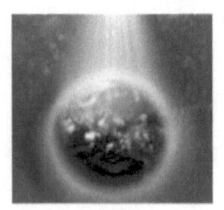

Pray for World Peace along with thousands of others every day at 09:09am and 09:09pm

Divine Light of Love, Bliss and Peace is Showering;
The Golden Light of Higher Consciousness is Rising;
All negativity on Earth is Dissolving;
Everyone is in Peace and Blissfully Shining;
O God, Gratitude for Everything!

www.ingramcontent.com/pod-product-compliance
Lightning Source LLC
LaVergne TN
LVHW041841070526
838199LV00045BA/1377